PRACTICAL STRATEGIES FOR THE MODERN ACADEMIC LIBRARY

Mike Heery and Steve Morgan

THE ASSOCIATION FOR INFORMATION MANAGEMENT

Published in 1996 by
Aslib, The Association for Information Management
Information House
20-24 Old Street
London
EC1V 9AP

***

A CIP Catalogue record for this book is available from the British Library
ISBN 0 85142 370 1

Aslib, The Association for Information Management, has some two thousand corporate members worldwide. It actively promotes better management of information resources.

Aslib lobbies on all aspects of the management of and legislation concerning information. It provides consultancy and information services, professional development training, conferences, specialist recruitment, and the Aslib Internet Programme, and publishes primary and secondary journals, conference proceedings, directories and monographs.

Further information about Aslib can be obtained from :
Aslib, The Association for Information Management
Information House, 20-24 Old Street, London, EC1V 9AP
Tel: +44 (0) 171 253 4488, Fax: +44 (0) 171 430 0514
Email aslib@aslib.co.uk, WWW http://www.aslib.co.uk/aslib/

Contents

Preface

Much has been written about the need for academic libraries to change. It is commonly stated that college and university libraries must develop in a way that meets the changing needs of further and higher education. But what does this mean in practice? What practical steps can academic librarians take to move in the required direction? The future – and in particular futuristic notions such as the electronic library or the library without walls – can seem remote. Yet librarians must begin to develop the services, the collections and the facilities of their libraries in an appropriate way. This is something for *all* academic librarians to address, and certainly not just those in more senior positions. Change is an issue for those who provide services as much as it is for those who plan them.

Change is needed in three important areas. Firstly librarians must become effective operators within parent organisations that are increasingly governed in a 'managerial' way. Secondly, they need to deal with and secure opportunities from the great range of educational changes that have taken place over the past five years and which are likely to continue. Thirdly, librarians must address all the issues that stem from technological change, and which include an inevitable shift of emphasis from policies concerned with holdings to those that promote access. If they are to succeed, librarians will have to learn new skills and develop new practices.

This book aims to identify specific areas where librarians can take practical steps to develop library services in ways that meet the needs of their changing environment. The book does not attempt to be comprehensive. In other words it is not a manual covering every aspect of academic librarianship. The book is concerned with those library services which we believe will be of critical importance in the coming years. The aims of the book are, therefore, ambitious, and the authors crave indulgence for what may appear to be an *over*-ambitious project! The ideas and proposals in this book are based upon our own experience, both at work and in our wider professional life. We have also learnt a great deal from the literature of academic librarianship, which – for the most part – continues to inform and to stimulate. We hope that both practising and prospective academic librarians will recognise in our approach a commitment to realistic developments in library services. We also hope that practising librarians will find within the book practical suggestions that are relevant to their own libraries, and that students will find the book useful as a source of information about academic librarianship in the 1990s.

1

The authors have benefitted enormously from innumerable discussions with colleagues at the University of the West of England and elsewhere. More specific thanks must go to Gill Burrington and the Burrington Partnership for the material on meetings used in Chapter 2; to all those librarians who provided the illustrative material contained in the appendices; and most especially to Ingrid Cox and Mary Takahama, whose secretarial and wordprocessing skills – not to mention their calm tolerance in the face of extra work – were essential in enabling us to complete the book.

Mike Heery and Steve Morgan

Bristol, March 1996.

1. Key Issues in the Modern Academic Library

'... higher education institutions need to reassess the position of libraries and librarians and their functions, clarify their objectives, and allocate resources to enable these to be met.' [1]

This book is written against a background of speculation about the future of academic librarianship. In the UK the Follett and Fielden reports have given an official blessing to suggestions that academic librarians need to develop new roles. [2] The *Follett Report* identifies some of the forces behind change in librarianship: the expansion of higher education; the development of an integrative, managerialist form of university governance; the necessity of recognising that all libraries need strategies for access to literature, rather than concentrating on collection-building. Above all Follett recognises the importance of information technology.

'The emergence of the electronic library and the widespread availability of eletronic information provide many opportunities to enhance the role of librarians in support of teaching and research.' [1]

The *Fielden Report* addresses the need to develop new skills in academic librarians in response to an environment of change. The strengths and weaknesses of the *Fielden Report* have been assessed by Parry. [3] However the *Fielden Report* is right in emphasising two important issues facing academic librarians. Firstly, the need to develop new skills in response to the changes sweeping higher education. For example, changes in teaching and learning, in organisational structures and in the importance of IT require that librarians develop a profile of skills that fit institutional needs. Secondly, the report rightly emphasises the importance of staff management in academic libraries. The staff development required of librarians, together with the need to deliver an effective range of new services, demand sound management abilities.

The purpose of this book is to provide practical ideas that are relevant to librarians keen to develop services that are appropriate to further and higher education institutions in the late 1990s. Much debate is heard of the new role of the librarian. Terms such as cybrarian, information navigator, knowledge counsellor, transformational librarian, information professional, information facilitator etc. have been coined in recent years in an attempt to define the new role of the librarian. [4]

Indeed, this debate is not confined to academic librarians. Librarians in a wide range of special libraries are experiencing a similar degree of organisational and technological change, and whilst it is a sad truth that the literatures of academic and special libraries seem quite separated, there is a lot that the two groups can learn from each other.

Whatever the need to redefine the role and terminology of librarianship, terms like cybrarian have a futuristic ring. Similarly, advocates of the virtual library suffer from a sense of their proposals applying to a future time that to many still seems remote. There can be a credibility gap between the claims of the futurists and the day-to-day experience of practising librarians. The mundane business of supplying texts to feed the voracious appetites of large undergraduate programmes, or the struggle to edit the collection of periodicals that supports researchers, contrasts with visionary thinking. There is a danger of some librarians adopting a jaundiced view of the claims of the futurists. This is captured well in the witty comment of the late Brian Enright that 'the paperless library is about as desirable as the paperless lavatory'. Luddism, however, has its own dangers.

The task that we have set ourselves in writing this book is that of suggesting ideas for development that are realistic enough to appeal to the overworked librarian but which will also help to steer the library's services in a direction appropriate to the changing times. We are all working in the here and now with all its familiar pressures. Our services need to evolve towards a new role in a way that is achievable within the constraints and opportunities of institutional realities. Our belief is that librarians need a clear sense of the strategic development of their library, and that this should guide the step-by-step development of specific library services. In other words, the services will move in the direction of a new role suited to future needs if we implement concrete changes in a realistic, achievable way. Librarians can certainly learn from each other, and this book attempts to draw upon 'best practice' in a wide range of academic libraries so as to build up a picture of how a modern library can operate.

The starting point for this book is, therefore, that academic libraries must develop and enhance the services they offer their users. Not to change is simply not an option. The force of change is irresistible. Modern societies and large organisations such as universities and colleges will continue to be subject to change. To some extent this is due to the political and economic forces that seem to have more impact on our lives with every decade. The interaction and growing competitiveness of the global economy will drive faster rates of change in all modern societies. In addition, organisations are increasingly subject to change that has a technological origin. As the rate of technological change accelerates organisations are forced to find ways of keeping pace. Educational bodies are affected just as much as commercial enterprises. This has serious implications for how institutions are organised – how they are structured and how they are managed. As the external environment becomes one of continuing change organisational life will also be subject to ongoing development. Organisations such as universities and colleges – and within them, libraries – will have to be managed in a way that can cope with and take advantage of an environment of change. Above all, organisations will need to be flexible, continually adapting to changing circumstances.

An important consequence of continuing change is that serious consideration must be given to the management of academic libraries. This book is primarily concerned with practical library matters that will support the development of a modern, service-oriented library. These practical developments will not happen on their own. Nor will they succeed solely through the efforts of enthusiasts. They need a properly planned and ordered environment, where changes are being addressed in a logical manner. In other words, they need to be well-managed. It is essential to consider the management of libraries at a time of change. How can library managers deliver the adaptable academic library?

The adaptable academic library will have certain key characteristics. These can be summarised under five headings, as follows:

- integration into institutional life
- strategic planning
- participative management
- service-orientation
- consultation.

Together, these five subjects comprise, for academic librarians, the effective management of change. Where these issues are addressed the library is more likely to develop, to innovate and to realise the new role that is appropriate to the changing times.

Integration into institutional life

It is increasingly important that university and college libraries are closely integrated into the academic life of their institutions. There are three reasons for this. Firstly, there is a growing need to demonstrate that the library uses resources in a way that is accountable to institutional management. Secondly, the adoption of an integrated educational role is the key to winning resources. Thirdly, integration is a prerequisite to effective strategic planning.

Accountability

As financial resources become tighter it can be seen that academic institutions are becoming more accountable to the government bodies that fund them. As part

5

of this process departments within universities and colleges have also become accountable to institutional management. All departments, including the library, are expected to provide value for money. This means that they are expected to spend their resources in a way that meets the needs of the institution. It is therefore important that the parent institution understands what its library is trying to achieve and how it is performing in practice. What are the library's strategies? How are they being implemented? Are they effective? These questions are relevant to everyone in the institution. After all, the library uses a considerable amount of the institution's money. It ought therefore to be accountable for its performance.

Increasingly, academic libraries are accountable not only to the institutional executive , but also directly to academic departments. This is especially true where new, more rigorous financial systems are introduced. In the UK in recent years institutional changes have often included the introduction of new methods of financial management. For example, the creation of an internal market between cost centres makes the library answerable in resource terms to those who use its services. Where the library is open to criticism by academic departments because it is perceived as unresponsive to changing needs it is likely to lose out in the annual cycle of resource allocation. In fact the demand that users of a service get value for their money from that service is not just a matter for financial managers. There is change afoot in society at large whereby everyone – including students – are becoming more assertive about what is perceived as bad service. A student population who complain regularly about their library will influence the opinions of those institutional managers who are responsible for allocating resources. It is essential that the library retain the support of institutional decision-makers.[5]

An educational role

The library that wishes to survive and prosper in changing times must be seen to have a real engagement with academic programmes. The worst possible outcome for the library is to be seen as remote and incomprehensible. The library must participate fully in the educational life of faculties. It can do this by playing an active part in all faculty meetings, including those where new courses are planned. The library must demonstrate to academic staff that it fully understands what they are trying to achieve; that it is organised so as to work in partnership with academic staff; and that it is using its initiative to play a full part in finding solutions to the problems that faculties face as a result of significant educational and organisational change.

In an environment of considerable change everyone is under pressure. There will be little sympathy for the librarian who is reduced to bleating about overwork or inadequate resources because academic staff and other departments will themselves be experiencing similar pressure. The only way forward for the library is to make positive proposals that meet the requirements of the new situation. For example, what should a library do about the growing number of off-campus students? Most established university libraries are clearly not organised to provide a service to students who never come to the university. So should the library just ignore them? The answer to this question must be no, the library cannot afford to ignore them. The library has to devise ways of helping these students, who after all have paid their fees and expect to get a good service in return. Where UK libraries *have* chosen to ignore distance learners there are examples of faculties themselves setting up library-like services to solve the problem – in effect marginalising the library. The library's response, therefore, has to be to take positive action, to produce realistic proposals that meet the needs of students, and in that way to secure the institutional support that is likely to lead to financial resources.

Librarians must, therefore, be credible in an educational role. They must be able to relate to their academic colleagues as equals. The final chapter of this book considers the individual qualities that innovative academic librarians might be required to possess. Here it will suffice to say that they must be as much at home in academic or pedagogical discourse as in that pertaining to IT or management. The culture of an academic institution derives primarily from educational practice; that is from the engagement of individuals with ideas in the activities of teaching, learning and research. The librarian who is successfully integrated into the parent institution will naturally be at home in the pervading educational culture (or indeed cultures, where the ethos of different disciplines can produce a varied institutional environment).

The librarian of the future may not, therefore, be wholly removed from the scholarly librarian of old. The modern academic librarian needs to retain a genuine interest in and aptitude for scholarly activity. This idea can be emphasised by describing the librarian as a professional who needs to have a close understanding of his or her client group. There needs to be sympathy between the two – a shared understanding and a realisation of the mutual benefits of the relationship between the two. The writings of John Kay are relevant here. Kay argues that professionals (like librarians) should have what he terms 'a relational contract' with their clients:

> 'The terms of the relationship are not written down, and often cannot be precisely articulated – hence the term implicit contract. And the relationship depends on trust between the parties and is – in the terms in which the word is commonly used – not a contract at all ... relational contracts suffer rather than benefit from too precise a specification of obligations.'[6]

Kay's ideas about the nature of a successful and effective relationship between the professional and his or her clients are relevant to academic librarians. We need to be seen as participators in the educational process. The crude quantitative contracts or service level agreements being advocated by some librarians are therefore out of place. They are foreign to the ethos of further and higher education. They hinder rather than help the librarian who wishes to be integrated into the educational life of the institution. The practicalities of academic integration are considered in Chapter 2.

Strategic planning

Management skills, such as strategic planning, are essential for the librarian faced with change. If change is not to be experienced as something that just happens to the library, with unknown consequences, the library must actively deal with new situations. Strategic planning is a tool for tackling change head on, in order to control it. In fact many of the changes taking place in post-compulsory education offer opportunities to libraries. These opportunities are more likely to be taken where the library employs carefully planned strategies with clear objectives.

In answer to the question 'Why plan?' Corrall states that '... planning helps us to prepare for a better future... strategic planning fulfils the dual role of relating an organisation and its people to the environment and providing unity and direction to its activities'. [7] The techniques of strategic planning help the manager to analyse the changing environment. For example, the librarian needs a clear analysis of both the current situation and how the institution is going to change over the next few years. What are our strengths and weaknesses? How will the forthcoming changes affect the library, and what should be done as a result? These questions can be answered by using strategic planning. This is because strategic planning is not an intellectual activity that is separate from day-to-day work. In a well-managed library strategic planning is an integral part of the day-to-day work. It facilitates the organisational responsiveness that is needed in a period of change. Corrall maintains that 'Strategic planning is a process in which purposes, objectives and plans are formulated, and then implemented; both formulation and implementation processes are evolutionary and continuous. It is a process of relating an organisation to its changing market opportunities, a key concern being the pressures, constraints, opportunities and threats within the sector in which it competes or operates'. In terms of academic libraries, the 'organisation' that Corrall refers to is the library, and the 'sector' is the parent institution.

Strategic planning requires the participation of staff. It is not a remote process. The senior managers of the library may have greater input into the analysis of the library's changing environment. However, staff at all levels should be involved in deciding upon specific goals and how to implement them.

'Academic libraries are complex organisations with interlocking and interdependent operations. They must rely on shared expertise and group problem solving if they are to operate with increased effectiveness and achieve their goals. Strategic planning processes create opportunities for staff at all levels of the organisation to inform themselves about the organisation and its environment and such processes empower them to work creatively and cooperatively to choose effective strategies and reach common agreement about goals.'[8]

Strategic management is not only relevant within the library. The formulation of a strategic plan is also important in relations with the wider institution. Many libraries are required to formulate a strategic plan as part of a wider planning process. They agree annual targets or planning agreements with the institutional executive. In one sense, therefore, the formulation of a strategic plan can simply be a part of how things are done across the institution. The planning process is most useful, however, where it helps to *influence* the institutional executive. It then provides a means of keeping library issues before institutional policy-makers and allows the librarian to show how library strategies relate to institution-wide strategies. It can help to tie the library closely into general institutional planning.

'Active engagement of campus faculty and administrators in discussions about library plans and services is especially important in times of fiscal austerity and in environments characterised by fierce competition for limited resources. Such discussions can lead to a new consensus or reaffirmation of the significance of the library's role within the academic environment.'[8]

Participative management

The implementation of strategic plans will be most effective where the library is managed in a participative way. The proliferation of change means that hierarchical or bureaucratic forms of administration will be unable to cope with the increasing number of decisions that have to be made. This is particularly true where the extent of technological change increases the complexity, as well as the degree, of decision-making. A library that wishes to implement continuing changes needs to be structured in a way that supports its objectives. This does not mean that a certain staff structure should be developed. It means that the actual process of management, regardless of the structure of line management, should be participative. Library staff need to be wholly involved in the decision-making process if the library is to manage on-going change effectively. It is inadequate to expect the head of department to make all key decisions. He or she will not be able to master all the information necessary to guide decision-making. The extent and the complexity of change are too great. This is especially true in a computerised environment, where staff responsibilities will become increasingly specialised. The collective knowledge of library staff is necessary to inform effective technological development. The answer must be that the library staff become involved in decision-making. Instead of one or two individuals – the 'great man' approach to leadership – the totality of the library staff must ensure that the library maximises the opportunities that arise in an environment of change.

Successful participative management has three important aspects. Firstly, those who run the library must be able to relate well to library staff at all levels. The overbearing, domineering personality has no place in successful management of staff. Social changes mean that staff will not respond at all well to rule by diktat – a simple truth that some head librarians seem unable to recognise. Most library staff are interested in their work and are keen to do well. They will respond positively to information about the environment around the library and about the decisions that have to be made. An atmosphere of sharing information, expressing opinions confidently and openly, and of constructive criticism is essential. The library needs to feed off the knowledge and creativity of all its staff. An ethos of participation is required.

Secondly, the library must be wholly committed to a thorough-going programme of staff development. Individuals need their personal development to be nurtured, through appraisal or some other process of individual feedback and encouragement. In addition, the library needs to invest in library-wide staff development so as to ensure that staff have the skills to operate effectively in a period of change. These skills will increasingly be not only IT skills, but also teaching skills, negotiating skills and communication skills (see Chapter 7). These staff roles are means by which effective integration into institutional life will be achieved. The library must prioritise the resourcing of staff development programmes, particularly in these key areas.

Thirdly, the library must find practical ways of delivering meaningful participation by staff. This can be done by organising the internal business of the library in an appropriate way. For example, at the University of the West of England (UWE) library the key policy-making forum is a meeting of eighteen staff (out of a total of 164). This is called the Library Policy Committee. It makes decisions on policy for itself, and has, for example, been known to reject the proposals of the head of library services. The committee has representatives from all grades of staff. However, by itself this will not deliver real participation from staff. It is therefore supplemented by meetings of groups of staff, where library assistants, subject librarians and assistant librarians can meet with their peers with complete freedom to discuss whatever is of interest to them. Part of their time will be spent discussing the policy proposals of the Policy Committee. When the Policy Committee meets, therefore, proposals have already had widespread discussion, and committee members can represent their constituencies in an effective way. There is a genuine input from all staff to the decisions made in the Committee. At UWE the staff development committee and the systems committee are also run in this way.

A further means of effecting participative decision-making is by means of staff working groups. The implementation of the objectives contained in the library's strategic plan can be assigned to groups of volunteers drawn from the staff. There are always sufficient numbers of people willing to join a small group of staff who will decide how the library will make progress on a specific objective. After all, such activity provides very good experience to staff who are seeking career development. It is evident that staff at all levels can contribute well to working groups. However, it is necessary firstly to provide training to participants on how meetings should be conducted to run effectively. No-one wants to waste time – this will only undermine the credibility of the exercise. The chair of a working group should be well-chosen and should be given support by library management should any difficulties arise. It is therefore vital that library staff at all levels are equipped with the necessary skills to participate effectively at meetings. The importance of participation in meetings in covered in Chapter 2. If working groups are given proper support they can cover quite important areas of development. For example, at UWE Library such groups are at present working on a rolling programme of surveys of users; a policy for supporting researchers; recommendations for the development of networked sources of information; a system for providing management information and an IT training programme. The amount of work undertaken by such groups is considerable yet also acts as a positive motivator in terms of staff morale. The groups contribute considerably to the library's ability to manage and implement change.

Service-orientation

The adaptable academic library is a service-oriented library. This may or may not mean that traditional ideas about collection building are retained. It does mean that the library devises new services that meet changing institutional needs. The library that is integrated into institutional life and which actively plans its future will inevitably propose initiatives on the level and kind of services that it offers its users.

First of all, it is worth considering what is actually meant by service-orientation. In the authors' view it means, above all else, that library staff spend *time* with users of the service. A service-oriented library is one where the information needs of users are satisfied by the library staff spending time with users in order to help them obtain the information they require. This commitment of time may take the form of a high quality enquiry desk service (see Chapter 4). However, it also encompasses the following:

- teaching and training users (Chapter 3)
- individual help to users (Chapter 4)
- services dedicated to the needs of specific groups of users (Chapter 5)
- IT support (Chapters 3 and 4).

The adaptable academic library will not offer services only in a reactive way. It is undeniably important to help those who come into the library with enquiries. However, it is also very important that the library assume a proactive role in the provision of services and it must promote its services energetically. This may include the production of written guides, handouts and other library literature. It will also take the form of regular daily lobbying and negotiating on behalf of the services being promoted. The library must also secure the right to spend time with students and academic staff to ensure that they become effective users of the library. For example, it is essential that user education programmes are put in place in a way that is tailored to the needs of particular courses. Such programmes will run throughout the year and will develop in tandem with the developing information needs of students as they progress through their course. The complexity of the modern library necessitates an effective teaching and training role for library staff. Chapter 3 offers guidance on providing successful user education programmes.

Active, integrated user education programmes need backup from staff who are readily accessible to both students and academic staff. The library should support user education with a continuous service of advice and help to individuals (see Chapter 4). Such individual contact – whether it be to staff pursuing research or to students researching a dissertation – would act as a kind of tutorial backup to the user education lectures and workshops. The availability of library staff who are interested in their clients is of critical importance. Research into the needs of mature students at the University of Glamorgan has found that:

> 'Library staff are amongst the most accessible of support staff... Students value staff who listen to them without making judgements, who spend time with them and who are willing to accept that they may not know 'basic' things. It seems appropriate that staff should be aware of the needs of mature students and of their perceptions of HE if they are to provide a service to them.'[9]

The service-oriented library will strive to develop new services to its clients. For example, services can be targeted at specific groups of users (see Chapter 5). These may be part-time students, research staff, students from overseas, distance learners, users with disabilities or academic staff interested in open learning methods. Where these services are effective they will be based upon library staff dedicated to spending time in the promotion, development and implementation of the service. Staff will be spending time helping the particular group using the special service. Where such services are offered the library clearly needs to plan the deployment of its staff very carefully. Special services will not work as well where additional duties are simply added to the existing responsibilities of staff. They will also need to be coordinated with more general library services. However, where targeted services *are* effective they can make a real impact within the institution. The library will be seen to be developing new services that meet changing institutional needs, which in our view is the best way for the library to win resources in a period of change.

The notion of library staff spending time supporting its users in an active way is also relevant to the emerging electronic library. Librarians are increasingly debating the role of their profession in the light of sweeping technological change. Universities are being prompted to ask whether the expensive, collection-based library is relevant in the electronic age. While one may exaggerate the rate of change – the book is unlikely to decline, but will share its former hegemony with a growing range of paperless information sources – it is important that academic librarians devise strategies for developing their role in an increasingly networked environment. They have to promote their role, and probably to some extent also to defend it.

These service considerations apply also to the development of the electronic library, which can be seen in the UK eLib programme (see Chapter 7), as well as in individual libraries that are at the forefront of IT development, such as Carnegie Mellon in the USA and Tilburg. The experience of the library in the University of Tilburg in the Netherlands is relevant to us all, as it is closer to the electronic library than any other academic library in Europe. The library, in addition to the normal services of an academic library, offers self-service issue terminals, databases of journal contents, transparent network navigation, large numbers of open access networked PCs, a very well integrated range of software, interactive instruction packages and an image bank. The technical developments at Tilburg are very impressive. However, also of interest are the organisational implications of those technological developments. It is clear from Tilburg that the electronic library is dependent upon library staff who are service-oriented in the way already outlined in this chapter. The users of the electronic library will require considerable help in order for them to make effective use of the complex array of IT services. They will need the *time* of library staff. They will need considerable training and they will need subsequent one-to-one support. The library will need to be highly service-oriented if it is to meet the needs of the electronic future. [10]

The service-oriented library may be the key model for the successful academic library of the future. However, it will not happen by itself. It will need to be actively and professionally developed by those running the library. The most urgent requirement from librarians in a period of change is that they adopt a real commitment to effective, modern forms of management. We are now not only librarians but also managers, and the successful management of change is the most important task facing us. This book advocates a positive strategic planning approach to academic libraries, together with a genuine commitment to participative decision-making and inclusive staff management, as being the key to successful management of change. As the future of libraries becomes less collection-based and more concerned with access to networks of information librarians will need to be very service-oriented. That can only be delivered where organisational structures are flexible and library staff are adaptable to change. It is just as important to us to understand organisational politics, to introduce policies for good customer care and to deploy our staff in a way that will integrate them into academic life as it is for us to keep abreast of technological developments in networked sources of information. The IT future of libraries often seems to predominate in our professional literature. Our ability to navigate through all the changes facing us requires an understanding of the wider organisational and managerial implications of living in a world of continuous change. By so doing academic librarians may yet develop a new professional role that meets the needs of the 21st century.

Consultation

This introductory chapter has raised a number of themes that are considered in succeeding chapters. It has also suggested ways of organising the library. It is appropriate to end on a subject that has a practical role in helping us to develop new services. Librarians need to build consultation with others into their day-to-day work. This can take several forms. The overall aim is to produce a continuous supply of information that will help guide the librarian who wishes to innovate.

Consultation within the library has been covered under the heading of participative management. Other forms of consultation are equally important. Firstly, it is necessary to consult with users of the library. The HEFCE report *The effective academic library.*[11] emphasises the measurement of user satisfaction as a key means of assessing an academic library. The information gathered from users will help librarians who are looking to develop the services they offer. Such information can take the form of surveys, suggestions books, course monitoring and evaluation and user group meetings. Whatever form it takes, library staff should ensure they understand the quality of the information gathered. It is vital to make direct contact with students and other users to discover how the library can support them in the most effective way possible. But how reliable is the information gathered? It is not appropriate to answer this tricky question here, and indeed the

HEFCE report itself acknowledges the difficulty of gathering such qualitative data. However, it is appropriate to state that librarians must base their decisions on information about the needs of their users, and that they must be professional in their approach to such activities. The growing use in libraries of market research methods and of computer software such as Priority Search Libra is encouraging. A case study in the use of such software at Kingston University has been described by Horrocks. [12]

The adaptable academic library is one which works closely with others. Within educational institutions librarians need to work not only with academic staff but also with other central services. A library service to users with disabilities will, for example, benefit considerably from collaboration with those who recruit students, such as an Admissions Department, and those who support students, such as the Student Services Department. The library needs to be integrated in this institution-wide sense so that it forms partnerships with other departments. This type of activity can result in improvements to service. It can also lead to the joint provision of services, or in joint bidding to funding agencies. For example, in the UK the Teaching, Learning and Technology Programme (TLTP) and the Access to Education programme are both initiatives that have seen libraries working in partnership with other departments. Libraries can form such partnerships with academic departments, with staff development units, with student services or with computer centres. Joint projects allow more to be achieved than any single department could manage, and often also produce a more attractive bid to funding agencies.

Chapter 6 considers cooperation with others in more detail. In particular it looks at how libraries can benefit from cooperation with people and organisations outside their own institution. We will always look for tangible benefits in any cooperative venture. However, it is important to emphasise that consultation with others is the chief means by which we get new ideas. The task facing the academic librarian is to move library services forward in the most appropriate and effective way. Progress needs to be grounded in realistic ideas that will work well in practice. Librarians need practical ideas. We can all learn from the experience and the experiments of others. Good practical ideas will often derive from consultation with our colleagues in other libraries. It is the purpose of this book that it too will have a role in suggesting ideas that will help librarians to develop the services that they offer.

References

1. Joint Funding Councils' Libraries Review Group. *Report.* Bristol: Higher Education Funding Council for England, 1993. (*Follett Report*)

2. Fielden, J. *Supporting expansion: a report on human resource management in academic libraries for the Joint Funding Councils' Libraries Review Group.* Bristol: HEFCE, 1993. (*Fielden Report*)

3. Parry, J. Supporting expansion: the future for library and information staff. *British Journal of Academic Librarianship 9*(3), 1994, pp.149–158.

4. Ojala, M. What will they call us in the future? *Special Libraries,* Fall 1993, pp.226–229.

5. Heery, M. New model librarians: a question of realism. *Journal of Librarianship & Information Science,* 25(3), pp137–142.

6. Kay, J. *Foundations of corporate success.* Oxford: Oxford University Press, 1989, pp.50–57.

7. Corrall, S. *Strategic planning for library and information services.* London: Aslib, 1994.

8. Butler, M. & Davis, H. Strategic planning as a catalyst for change in the 1990s. *College & Research Libraries,* 53(5), 1992, pp393 – 403.

9. O'Donohoe, S. *et al.* Mature students: counselling and guidance needs – a role for libraries and learning resources providers. *Learning Resource Journal,* 18(2), 1992, pp40–43.

10. Geleijnse, H. A library of the future. *Library Association Record Technology Supplement,* 96(2), February 1994, pp10–11.

11. Joint Funding Councils' Ad-hoc Group on Performance Indicators for Libraries. *The effective academic library: a framework for evaluating the performance of UK academic libraries.* Bristol: Higher Education Funding Council for England, 1995.

12. Horrocks, A. Kingston University Library: survey of user preferences. *COPAL Newsletter,* 61, May 1993, pp.64–69.

2. Academic Integration

'Proactive analyst, subject expert, counsellor, consultant, linker, and inter-mediary in the cycle of scholarly endeavor and scholarly communication'

Description by Veaner of academic librarians in their liaison role.[1]

What is academic integration and why is it desirable?

It is sometimes easy to lose sight of the reasons for having academic integration as a goal. The overriding rationale behind this convergence between library service and institution – via departments, schools, faculties and other support services – must be ultimately the provision of a more effective service to the academic community. Such an approach is fully supported by the Follett and Fielden Reports. [2,3] As we shall see, liaison between library and department inevitably involves a variety of activities which, taken together, should help to cement a close relationship between the two constituents and thereby increase the likelihood of their needs being met.

Before considering the various liaison activities which together comprise the academic integration, we should ask – what is academic integration and why is it desirable ?

In the context of academic librarianship we have defined academic integration as:

> the nurturing of an active partnership between the library, academic departments and other institutional services in a wide range of liaison activities which respond to the information needs of the academic community.

Different nomenclature has been adopted by other parties: Fielden [3] has referred to 'academic convergence' which in the UK at least may be confused with the coming together of library and computing services specifically. We believe that academic integration encompasses both a different and a wider context. Horton [4], Holbrook [5], Miller [6] and Schloman *et al.* [7] have all used the term 'faculty liaison' – the preferred term in the US. In our view liaison activities refer to the means by which academic integration is achieved.

So why is academic integration a desirable objective? As Figure 2.1 shows, the ideal relationship between the institutional constituents resembles a continuous dialogue which ultimately benefits the users – whether students or staff.

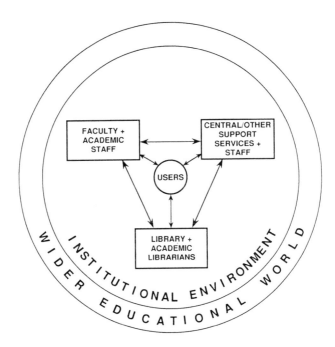

Figure 2.1 Main Constituents In Academic Integration

This tightly-integrated framework is desirable for the following main reasons:

Planning

Integration facilitates both short-term and long-term planning. Examples of the former are collaboration over lecturers' reading lists or restricting the loan of material for seminar work. Early involvement in course planning together with some input into the validation process can often lead to fruitful long-term relationships.

Finance

Continued stringency in resource provision puts added pressure on librarians to ensure that money is spent effectively. Academic integration increases the likelihood of this happening. Even if the financial situation improves, academic integration can act as a valuable model for the future.

Sharing knowledge and expertise

All parties within the integration process bring a diverse range of knowledge, skills and expertise. For maximum effect these should be pooled whenever possible. For example, academic staff bring knowledge of course assessment, teaching and learning skills; library staff bring a host of transferable skills, knowledge of the ways in which students study and learn across the board as well as familiarity with information technology developments; other support services provide counselling skills, knowledge of employment requirements, reprographic and multimedia skills. In the ideal situation these services will provide the academic community with their coordinated support.

Customer focus

Academic integration concentrates on satisfying the needs of the academic staff and students – the customers, consumers, users, clients or patrons. They are the focus – directly or indirectly – of the liaison activities described below. Involvement in seeking feedback from them is important, particularly with the continued movement to more independent approaches to learning.

Library profile

Academic integration can provide a vehicle for increasing the library's profile within the institution and for promoting its benefits as an integral part of the learning process rather than as an after-thought.

What follows are some illustrations of the results that can be achieved through academic integration.

Outcomes of academic integration

Firstly, one effective method of 'having a dialogue' with students is to channel information through the academic staff. This indirect approach may happen consciously or subconsciously. For example, in the former case the staff/student committee meeting at which the librarian is present may act as an appropriate vehicle for discussion of numbers of copies of books, restricted loans or other ongoing concerns. At a subconscious level a series of workshops organised for academic staff and covering perhaps new databases will eventually percolate down to students as the staff become familiar with these new services (this is assuming they do, of course!). Secondly, the increased coherence which effective liaison brings to the library/institution interface provides greater credibility in the eyes of students and staff. Activities such as participation in course planning and curriculum development, provision of subject-based guides and bulletins, presenting a paper on the moves to student-centred learning at a faculty meeting all provide opportunities to demonstrate a professional approach to assisting in the achievement of departmental or institutional goals. For students the integration of academic and library staff may be manifest in a programme of study jointly delivered and spread throughout the academic year or semester in a number of separate but connected information skills sessions. Such a programme would be difficult to plan, deliver and evaluate without the close cooperation of all parties. This vital area of teaching and learning is addressed in Chapter 3.

Academic integration can often act as a suitable vehicle for the library to partici-pate in the educational process. We believe that the attitudes exemplified in the research of Divay *et al.* [8] are declining in the 1990s – 'librarians are not com-monly viewed as contributing greatly to the overall educational process' or 'fac-ulty members do not recognise the academic role that librarians are contractually obliged to fulfil'. For example, if the library wants a particular topic to be dis-cussed or debated at the departmental level, the appropriate mechanism should be in place for this to happen. To take the example further, if the librarian needs to raise the issue of the modularisation of courses and its implication for support services, the discussion should be fitted into the cycle of departmental meetings at a suitable point. Similarly, should the librarian want to garner views on the services to students with disabilities and perhaps to raise the profile of the topic, the committee structure should facilitate such discussion.

Academic integration provides an effective means of communication. Across a spectrum between contacting a member of the academic staff on electronic mail to letting him or her know a particular book is available (or indeed presenting a paper at a course evaluation meeting about library user surveys) it is essential that the two parties communicate often and effectively regardless of the means. The faculty librarian is often perceived as representing the library in the faculty and the faculty in the library, fighting his or her corner when necessary. The role is viewed at times – rather unfairly – by users as 'an all-purpose nanny to whom any problem may be given', as Quiney [9] observed. The librarian will sometimes view educational events or developments differently from the academic staff and this needs to be aired. A good example is course planning. Modules, options, whole courses are proposed or even validated by professional or other bodies with little or no consideration of their resource implications. It is at this point that the librar-ian contributes to the debate – forcefully where necessary – in terms of the re-sources required for collection development, electronic sources, information skills sessions etc. The alternative is that at these events the academic machinery has built up such a momentum that the proposals or validations are carried forward regardless of the implications for central support services. The librarians merely take the flak when the students later find themselves in difficulty over an under-resourced (and possibly over-subscribed) course.

Liaison activity can be useful in focusing on specific information-related issues, for example reference and enquiry services, integrating networking facilities into programmes of study, and self-service issuing systems. It is helpful to know that a suitable structure or forum is firmly in place to explore these issues or at least begin a dialogue for future action.

Involvement by library staff in not only departmental matters but also in wider institutional activities often has the effect of improving the image of the library –

assuming that such involvement makes certain people sit up and listen. Atkinson [10] has done some interesting work on the image of the academic librarian. Participation may also heighten the existing knowledge base about current library and information matters and, if necessary, raise the library's profile. Examples of such involvement – which is one of the recommendations of the *Follett Report* [2] – would be preparation for and participation in Further Education Funding Council (FEFC) inspections, Higher Education Funding Council (HEFC[E]) research and teaching assessment exercises or Higher Education Quality Council (HEQC) audits. Although the same process applied to departmental liaison work should produce similar consequences, the infrequency of institutional events requires greater preparation and planning to achieve a similar impact. In any of these activities one must be continually conscious of the marketing opportunities which are provided.

Although experience suggests that attempts to integrate departmental and support services benefit the academic community, inevitably there are some downsides. The main problem associated with academic integration is the time factor. The weight of student numbers and the increasing administration and financial constraints contribute to the erosion of time for those working in post-compulsory education. Library and information services are no exception. Finding time to devote to these activities is often difficult. But ways must be found to ensure that the considerable time necessary for liaison work is as fruitful as possible for example effective time management – particularly where meetings are concerned, honing of communication and other interpersonal skills, and production of high quality literature.

Associated with the problem of time management is the culture of the organisation and its susceptibility (particularly on the part of the senior management) to facilitating liaison work. A library whose organisational culture is represented by a high rate of participation and whose management style is open and democratic will set the foundation for effective relationships.

It needs to be recognised that the nature of liaison work requires that the library be suitably staffed both quantitatively and qualitatively. Sufficient support staff need to be available to compensate for these time-consuming activities. Also, most importantly, staff need to be suitably skilled, with the appropriate qualifications, attitudes and interpersonal skills to make a success of this type of role. Attractive salaries, contracts and conditions of service will help to entice the right calibre of candidate.

User education has a significant part to play in the integration process. This is addressed in Chapter 3.

Academic integration in practice

We have identified four areas in which effective liaison work can be played out. It is not the intention to be comprehensive since library staff are always finding new and innovative ways of improving the relationship between them and the academic establishment. We have included those areas which have in our experience been the most fruitful sources of success. Whilst these have been categorised for ease of coverage, there will be inevitable overlaps. These are the four areas:

- meetings
- promotion
- publications
- institution-wide liaison.

'Meetings bloody meetings'

This title of a very expensive but thought-provoking video starring John Cleese implies that for many people meetings are a chore which should be avoided – a waste of time, unproductive, an interruption in the normal working day. It is perhaps summed up in the poster (figure 2.2). You will no doubt have your own views. We believe that meetings – regardless of content, participants, location or purpose – should be viewed as opportunities. The importance of effective meetings in the educational environment cannot be overstated. It is for this reason that a large proportion of this chapter is devoted to the task of helping ensure such effectiveness.

It can be all too easy to attend any meeting, sit back, remain passive, provide the occasional comment, at times allowing the discussion to wash over you and at the end move on to the next task on your busy schedule without a moment's reflection. Under these circumstances attendance may be largely a waste of time. The meetings referred to are those where three or more people are participating. Types of meetings (including informal ones) are dealt with later in the chapter. Having ascertained that the meeting is the most appropriate vehicle for your purpose (perhaps a memo, e-mail, face-to-face or telephone call may be more appropriate?), it is wise to consider the following elements for success:

- preparation
- participation
- follow-up procedures
- chairing.

Are You Lonely?
Work On Your Own?
Hate Having to Make Decisions?

THEN HOLD A MEETING

You Can Get To See Other People, Sleep In
Peace, Offload Decisions, Feel Important And
Impress (Or Bore) Your Colleagues

And All In Work Time

MEETINGS
THE PRACTICAL ALTERNATIVE
TO WORK

Figure 2.2

Preparation

Meetings often suffer through lack of preparation. Before attending a departmental meeting, for example, it is advisable to be well-briefed. Although this may be viewed as simple common sense, it is surprising how often hard-pressed staff fail at this first hurdle. Whilst understandable, a just-in-time approach including preparation five minutes before, on the way to the meeting or at the meeting (particularly tabled papers) is not recommended as best practice. One of the worst feelings of the librarian at a meeting is to feel unprepared when invited to comment on a specific topic. A well-briefed individual will attend a meeting in a more self-confident manner and is more likely to participate effectively. Briefing may take the form of:

- reading minutes of previous meetings
- ensuring that any agreed action has been taken or is in train

23

- thinking about the agenda and marshalling one's own thoughts on the topics in question

- reading any accompanying papers and forming views based upon them.

Naturally, if you are presenting a paper, good presentational skills are an essential prerequisite.

It may also be helpful, if required, to contact other participants for further information or clarification. If the meeting's objective is to make certain decisions, then the ability to argue a collective case from a position of strength becomes vital. An example would be a faculty meeting where the results of a course monitoring and evaluation survey show the library service in a bad light. The librarian may wish to approach other faculty representatives to discuss how to tackle the issue. Such a dialogue will help either to clarify the right approach (a political lever for increased resources ?), to 'get a feel for' the likely mood of the meeting's participants or to liaise with other support services represented.

Participation

Successful meetings need participation. Merely to attend and treat them as information-receiving exercises is to waste the opportunity of taking an effective part in the decision-making process. A number of more formal committees and boards put the library as a regular item on the agenda. If this is not possible or inappropriate, having a good rapport with the secretary, minute-taker or other suitable person is advisable so that items may be placed on the agenda when necessary. A regular spot on certain influential committees cannot be stressed enough. This ensures:

- a platform for discussion of specific library issues

- that participants are not surprised by the library's appearance on the agenda and try to foist on the meeting all their accumulated library-related problems (unless, of course, this is part of the meeting's remit)

- that a rapport may be established between library and other constituents

- an opportunity for the librarian to gain confidence practising presentation (amongst other) skills, speaking in a sometimes intimidatory environment

- the provision of a two-way communication channel so that departmental issues may be fed back to the library

- an opportunity to enhance the credibility, professionalism and image of the service

Although opportunities for participation may be provided, they are not always taken up. There could be a number of reasons for this. The librarian may:

- be an introvert personality to whom speaking out at such meetings does not come naturally
- lack knowledge about the topic under discussion
- be afraid to speak for fear of making a fool of him/herself
- feel excluded from an 'academic' club
- feel intimidated by the over-participation of certain dominating individuals and withdraw from the discussion.

There are no magic solutions to removing some of these barriers. Often the librarian needs to bite the bullet and be positive. Lack of knowledge could be rectified by more detailed preparation and requesting clarification – there will inevitably be someone who wants the same clarification as you but is afraid to show his or her ignorance. In our view 'making a fool of oneself' is a rather overrated fear. People are doing this all the time. It is an effective way of learning. Your own feelings of foolishness appear highly accentuated to you, when often other participants have not noticed your embarrassment or have immediately forgotten it. It is also worth remembering that:

- your comments may turn out to be sensible, accurate, informative or innovative, or thought-provoking
- you are entitled to express your views even though others may disagree with and argue against your opinions.

Assertiveness skills and a good relationship with the chairperson will invariably solve the problems of exclusivity and intimidation. Training courses covering the acquisition of these skills are available through bodies such as Aslib. Increasingly libraries also buy-in external trainers to teach these skills. An effective chairperson will encourage participation from those not doing so and also manage those personalities who try to dominate.

Advice on participation

- Speak early in the meeting if possible to gain self-confidence and facilitate later participation (otherwise the opportunity may slip away or someone else may make your point)
- have brief notes at hand and add to them in the meeting as appropriate (perhaps by the use of 5 x 3 inch cards which shows preparation and provides a structure)

- speak clearly and to all present (rather than to one or two individuals), making eye contact

- state your key message at the beginning of your contribution and make it positive where possible

- keep the language simple and avoid library jargon

- make one point at a time (there is sometimes a danger of trying to make a number of points simultaneously and ending up making no impact at all)

- provide evidence to support facts and opinions

- sentences should be short, punchy and expressed firmly

- after lengthy contributions it is helpful to summarise the points made for reinforcement and impact

- conceal any nerves by not having anything in your hands, for example notes, papers, pen, or glasses

- use controlled emotion for example by appropriate mix of smiling and serious expressions, without shouting or hectoring, but avoid becoming emotional

- become accustomed to catching the chairperson's eye (in the more informal environment it can be more difficult to interject but the briefest of lulls in the proceedings will usually suffice).

Whenever possible and appropriate, the librarian should make contributions to discussions on issues not directly related to the library service. It is important to show an understanding of how the service fits into the broader context of post-compulsory education and this is one opportunity to do so. Many topics have indirect implications for the support services for example assessment methods, semesterisation, modularisation, or equal opportunities. The librarian should be encouraged to put forward the library's views and also his or her own views on these issues. Preparation for such topics would include reading the professional and educational press as well as discussions with appropriate academic staff and library colleagues.

With the emphasis on active participation the importance of listening skills should not be forgotten. It is sometimes easy – particularly in a meeting which has become bogged down in minutiae or one in which the topic stands way outside your sphere of interest – to hear but not listen effectively. Listening requires an active approach which can take the form of:

- making notes of key points

- clarifying points by questioning

- noting what is *not* said (this is easier when well-prepared)

- constantly reflecting on your agreement or disagreement with points being raised

- observing dissonance between words and body language.

As already mentioned, participation at meetings does not necessarily come naturally or easily to some people. It represents a set of transferable skills which students are learning increasingly as part of their college and university curricula through seminar work, team-building exercises and other student-led approaches.

Follow-up procedures

All too often at the end of a meeting the issues and the meeting itself are soon forgotten. This is a mistake. There are a number of actions which may need to be carried out after the event. Always at the back of one's mind lurks the time factor. The following action points may be necessary:

- write up minutes if appropriate

- revisit notes made at meeting

- evaluate meeting either formally (see Appendix 1) or informally by reflecting (did the meeting achieve its objective? did I make a useful contribution? was I intimidated?)

- take any agreed action or at least note it in your list of priorities for future action

- brief colleagues or others who need to know any of the meeting's outcomes

- insert into diary date and venue of next meeting if appropriate.

What should definitely not be part of the post-meeting activity is to give your own views to participants or other colleagues instead of giving them *at the meeting*. This is a recipe for frustration, irritation, and annoyance.

Chairing meetings

You may be called upon to chair a committee, meeting or other working group with library and departmental representation. This task is often perceived as rather daunting. This need not be the case.

The chairperson's main role is to guide the meeting through the agenda to a successful conclusion. For very formal meetings the chairperson will need to be familiar with the group's constitution, rules, regulations and other protocols. Again appropriate preparation will ease the burden.

Having opened the meeting, made any introductions, outlined its purpose and indicated a proposed completion time, the chairperson guides the meeting through both controlling and letting the discussion flow. Facilitation of this activity requires control in broad areas:

Procedures
1 keep to the agenda; do not add to it unless it is vital; if necessary, make use of Any Other Business

2. keep to time; have a notional amount for each topic and try to stick to it; it may need to be expressed (i.e. 10 minutes for this topic)

3. keep to each issue; do not allow people to hijack or divert issues

4. make decisions when necessary

5. agree actions; ensure these are to be done by appropriate people.

Processes
1. facilitate discussion; involve all participants; encourage different views; use eye contact to persuade.

2. use methods appropriate to the meeting, for example brainstorming or nominal groups.

3. encourage constructive comments.

Difficult people or difficult situations
There will be occasions when the chairperson needs to be firm but gentle, for example someone rambles at length, makes vague suggestions, keeps interrupting or talking to the person next to him or her, dominates the meeting or makes derisive comments. There is a variety of ways by which the chair can resolve such difficulties, for example, by asking those who are being overshadowed by particularly talkative individuals to give their point of view. Most times participants will be supportive of your actions because they want the meeting to have a successful outcome and because people are generally cooperative.

Types of meeting

There is a wide range of meetings that take place under the aegis of liaison work and in which librarians should take a full part. Some examples are the following – the nomenclature will vary.

• Department/Faculty/School meetings

• Library/Learning Resources Committee

• Academic Board

- monitoring/evaluation
- course validation
- course planning
- course management
- course review
- teaching and learning
- media resources
- support services
- Staff/Student Forum
- Library Advisory Group
- quality assurance
- quality assessment
- Research Committee
- Library Users' Group.

Clearly, libraries will vary in their representation at such meetings. For some people it may be difficult, if not impossible, to gain access to any of the meetings taking place at the library/departmental interface. Indeed some may either have abandoned any effort to do so or see few benefits in devoting time to such activities. For others the problem may lie in the plethora of meetings and the choice as to which to attend for maximum benefit. Those who wish to participate in particular meetings would be advised to send a formal note to the chairperson, leader or other appropriate person explaining the reasons for the request. Whether this note should be provided by the senior management of the library or the librarian him or herself (this may of course be the same person) is a matter for individual judgement. If the meeting is of a more formal nature and part of the institution's decision-making structure, then notification is best coming from the senior management. Should such requests fall on deaf ears, it may be wise to:

- provide details of other similar institutions where this arrangement works effectively
- make a direct approach to the institution's senior management
- lobby other members of the appropriate committee(s) to support your inclusion.

Much determination on the library's part may be required to effect the necessary cultural shift. The incremental approach whereby the closed door gradually becomes ajar seems to be the most likely strategy for success. Some libraries may be in the healthy position of having representations on a number of committees. The problem then is to choose to attend those which make the most effective use of staff time. At least by having representation you will more than likely receive all the necessary papers and will know the topics for discussion. Thus armed you will be able to make an informed choice about attendance.

Informal meetings

Although this chapter has so far concentrated on more formal meetings, the importance of informal meetings should not be forgotten. Much valuable liaison work is carried out or instigated in corridors, refectories, bars, staff rooms, car parks, on the stairs or during meetings. It can be guaranteed from personal experience that a librarian walking (even purposefully) along the corridors of departments will be stopped for a quick chat which develops into more specific issues, for example advice about a CD-ROM, arranging a date for a discussion on journal subscriptions, putting material on restricted loan etc. Also, with the widespread adoption of e-mail limited meetings may be held at a distance.

Another type of meeting which sometimes comes under this umbrella (although it can also be a formal and structured process) is the staff/student or library/student forum. These gatherings provide users with the opportunity to quiz the academic and/or library staff about their courses and support services. These may require the library representative to be well-versed in the art of diplomacy and highly-skilled in assertiveness; the 'troubleshooting ombudsman' is perhaps a polite description of such a role. However, these do provide the opportunity for the librarians to put their side of the argument and, if necessary, place the library in a (more) positive light. One piece of advice at such meetings is to avoid saying you are going to investigate a problem and then fail to report back. It is important to take time to investigate matters if the trust and cooperation of the users and the staff are to be fostered.

In place of using library committees in some institutions it is through a series of library representatives – perhaps one person representing each department or faculty – that valuable liaison work may be carried out. Library representatives may find it useful to restrict their activities to a small number of specific areas. Such areas could include:

- book selection
- journal subscriptions
- database purchase and evaluation
- reading lists
- collection development

- budgetary matters
- user education
- changes in library practices
- support for research
- services for new academic staff
- departmental changes.

In conclusion, it may help those people who favour 'soundbites' as a method of remembering to ponder on these eight tenets:

1. meeting skills can be learned.
2. meeting skills need to be practised.
3. meetings need appropriate leadership.
4. meetings need work by all participants.
5. meetings need clear objectives.
6. meetings should have clear outputs.
7. meetings need auditing.
8. meetings can be enjoyable.

Promotion

The proactive approach – publicising and promoting services, facilities and products – forms a vital part of the liaison work between librarian and department. Although on the surface such an approach may appear to be using a one-way channel of communication, for the purposes of public relations this is not the case. In reality this type of promotion can act as a catalyst in establishing a dialogue between the two constituents. Where an effective relationship already exists, such activity will act as a vehicle for a continuation of the dialogue. A *sine qua non* of successful liaison work lies in the regularisation of contact through a variety of methods and vehicles.

Workshops

It is important that workshops are organised in such a way as to maximise the attendance. Not surprisingly attendance rates can be low when the location is too far away, the event is timed to clash with some other activity or the content is somehow unattractive. If these basic arrangements have been established, there is a greater chance of success. The busy academic has many competing calls on his or her time. Workshops must therefore demonstrate that they are of real benefit.

The workshop represents an effective means whereby academic staff are able to update or improve their knowledge and skills in library and information services. Periodically complaints are heard that some academic staff perpetuate outmoded ideas about available services. One possible way of remedying these attitudes would be to encourage attendance at and participation in such workshop events. Regularly organised they become a recognised part of the academic calendar which should not be allowed to become stale.

Practical Advice on Organising Workshops

- plan the event well in advance including rooms, equipment, intended participants and refreshments

- publicise the event well in advance so that academic staff may note dates in rapidly-filling diaries

- publicity needs to be of a high standard so that potential participants receive the 'right messages' about the event – a professional approach

- publicise events through a variety of methods so that there can be no excuse for not knowing – the so called 'belt and braces' approach. Example methods would include electronic mail, bulletin boards, mailshots, staff room notice boards, memos, telephone, word of mouth and newsletter

- ensure the time is right. Avoid times of high pre- or post-examination activity and, some would suggest, Wednesday afternoons (student sport and leisure periods) when the competition for academic attention is particularly high. If departments hold staff development events, whether single days or longer periods, reading weeks, inter-semester breaks etc. it may be possible to include a workshop as part of a larger programme of events. The closer the relationship with the department becomes, the easier will such an event be to timetable in this way. In many institutions academic staff development activities are regarded as compulsory with attendance expected to be high. This provides the potential for a captive audience

- ensure that the length of the workshop fits its purpose. Too short and you will fail to include everything you intended to; too long and staff will (a) not allow themselves the time and therefore not turn up or (b) leave midway through and perhaps cause an incremental exodus

- the importance of targeting the audience should not be underestimated. For example, sending publicity or promotional material to inappropriate staff has the effect of not only wasting your time and their time but also of potentially alienating those staff from attending future library-related events

- make yourself available not just during but immediately after the event.

This time can be spent fruitfully discussing with the participants any issues arising out of the workshop (or indeed any matter peripheral to or even unconnected with it!). This provides the opportunity for further liaison activity

- evaluate the events whenever possible. This may be done through question-naires, e-mail, follow-up telephone calls or even just through your own observations

- consider organising and running a workshop jointly with appropriate rep-resentatives from academic departments

- ensure the location is right. Checks on equipment such as computers, flipcharts, overhead projectors, screens, furniture and room arrangements are advisable. Experience teaches that machinery and other inanimate ob-jects that have been behaving themselves thus far will take on a totally different (and disruptive) guise. Liaison with other support services may be necessary particularly in terms of computer and IT back-up

- call on the help and support of the library staff. Firstly, colleagues should be informed about any events that are taking place. This action is likely not only to assist the smooth organisation and running of workshops but also to disseminate examples of good practice within the library environment. Shar-ing of ideas is always to be encouraged. The organisational and presentational skills of the library staff involved are likely to be tested to the full

The types of workshops which may be useful promotional vehicles include the following:

- updating on existing but underused services

- updating on services which are cross-disciplinary or cross-departmental. This could be shared by appropriate library staff and may be thematic. Particular attention needs to be paid to targeting audiences in this case

- updating on multimedia or other IT services perhaps involving other sup-port services

- publicising major alterations to existing services.

- publicising new services

- publicising existing services

- publicising existing services to staff other than departmental academic staff such as administrative staff, central staff, support staff, staff at associated/ affiliated/neighbouring institutions, particular types of staff – part-time, temporary, research etc.

The organisation of workshops for students is covered in Chapter 3.

Demonstrations

Whilst workshops are generally interactive events, demonstrations tend to be more of a one-way channel of communication. Often the two types of event overlap so that demonstrations may be followed by the opportunity to gain practical experience of the products or system on show. Such demonstrations may be usefully organised by librarians to publicise and promote particular new services, for example CD-ROM or full-text databases, a document delivery service, or a new type of technology. Invariably, commercial organisations are only too eager to cooperate by arranging for representatives to promote their products at suitable venues. It may be the case that the library has purchased or subscribed to a service part of whose cost will support training and demonstrations. Interested parties could be invited accordingly.

As with workshops the provision of suitable refreshments will generally encourage a healthy attendance.

Induction for new academic staff

The support services will play an important part in the life of new academic staff but realistically their place in the list of priorities will vary from half-way down to somewhere near the bottom. It will augur well for the future and establish a good initial working relationship if the first meeting with new academic staff is a fruitful one. The foundation is thereby laid for future liaison activities.

Whether new staff are inducted within an institutional programme, an *ad hoc* programme, an individual programme or some other arrangement, the library needs to be involved. As with induction for students it is preferable that the process is divided into an initial introductory session followed by a more detailed meeting. The latter will focus on the interests of the individual member of staff and build a solid platform for later cooperation.

Practical advice on induction for new academic staff
- seek names of new staff as early as possible and find out what arrangements have already been made for them. This assumes that the library is not already included

- if necessary, arrange a library session that dovetails into an existing programme. Failing that, arrange to meet with new staff individually.

- ensure that these arrangements coincide with their other induction commitments. It should be timed appropriately – if possible, to fit in with their notional priority list. If the meeting is too soon after arrival, much of the detail will be lost or make little impact. If it is left too long, the person will become heavily committed in other teaching or research areas and may be unable to devote sufficient time to induction

- at the first meeting ensure that the new member of staff is given the appropriate number and types of support literature. It is preferable to publicise only those services which are likely to be of immediate need. The rest should be left until later making specific arrangements where required

- at the first meeting find out teaching/research interests so that subsequent sessions may focus on specific services and facilities.

Open days and visits

At universities and colleges various promotional events take place in which libraries may participate. There are a number of reasons why this can be an effective liaison activity:

- the library is perceived as an integrated part of the teaching and learning process. It is viewed as an important support service

- it provides an opportunity to project and enhance the image of the library not only to the attendants at the event but also to the academic staff and other institutional staff involved

- the library can be a positive selling point. In terms of an open day to attract new students the library represents just one of the many elements to be weighed up . Potential students will be considering the institution as a package. The support services may provide the competitive advantage required to tip the balance; at the very least it will make a (hopefully) positive contribution to the overall impression

- it is encouraging for potential students to know that there will be copious amounts of assistance when attending the institution. They will benefit from the reassurance that they are not alone in what is sometimes a traumatic and daunting step.

If the library is not included in the programme, the librarian should set in train the process whereby a tour, demonstration, five minute talk, package of handouts, or indeed whatever seems appropriate, are provided.

Publications

Any effective relationship between the library and the department will no doubt be accompanied by a variety of publications. Such publications are provided for many purposes, some of which are:

- to provide a specific information service to a group of academic staff

- to provide support material for particular services and facilities

- to publicise the library and new and updated services

- to provide a current awareness and alerting services (see Chapter 4)

- to enhance the library's image.

Such publications will not only provide valuable services in their own right but also act as a catalyst for dialogue between library and department. It therefore represents another means of bolstering a flagging relationship, oiling the wheels of a flourishing one or initiating a new relationship – perhaps as one element within a broader strategy.

Nowadays it is quite possible to produce inexpensive printed publications of very high quality. The widespread use of desktop publishing software and other pc-based products together with improvements in reprographic technology have ensured such quality. Even if the library and information services themselves do not possess the facilities or the expertise, then it is likely that central support services will be able to provide them. Increasingly prevalent use is being made of information technology to provide these publications not only in printed form but also via e-mail. Problems may arise where different modes of delivery are needed by different groups. For example, some academic staff may have postponed the task of familiarising themselves with e-mail processes – for whatever reasons. These may include lack of priority, a Luddite tendency, or lack of time. Some staff may therefore receive a regular list of new book acquisitions via their e-mail boxes whilst others may have requested printed copies.

The costs of publication – in terms of staff time and materials – should be borne in mind. Depending on the purpose, frequency, content, quality and number of copies of a document, the output has to be monitored to ensure that the benefits accrued from production are worth the costs involved. Many of the publications like many other elements of the library service lend themselves to evaluation. It may be discovered, for example, that a regular newsletter is read or scanned by only a small number of the targeted audience. Is it therefore worthwhile persevering with the service? The reasons for its non-use may lie in uninteresting contents, unattractive layout or unhelpful format as well as a lack of time on the part of academic staff. An evaluative exercise could provide such helpful data.

The different kinds of publication provided by academic library services are manifold. The support material which accompanies the teaching and learning process is included in Chapter 3. Below is a selection of guides found in most library services and which could be targeted at the academic staff. New acquisitions and journal contents pages are considered in Chapter 4.

Guides

- general library guides: these may be guides to one campus/site or to the library services across the institution. Basic details are provided including loans, opening hours, study areas, contacts and maps
- subject guides: these may be guides to areas of study including discrete subjects or cross-disciplinary themes. The latter are becoming more prevalent as the boundaries between hitherto unconnected areas blur and as programmes of study are taught by teams taken from a number of different departments. Such guides may include location numbers, lists of journals, reference material and databases. They may range from one side of A4 paper to more substantial publications incorporating literature searching techniques or referencing systems. Such guides also range from the purely descriptive to the highly evaluative, from the superficial to the more in-depth
- guides to specific services or for specific categories of user: these may include interlibrary loan or other document delivery services, library catalogues, short loan, undergraduate or other special collections, audiovisual and media resources; services to part-time, disabled, distance learning, placement students, those studying at associated institutions and other categories of nontraditional users are included in Chapter 5
- guides to electronic sources: the proliferation of new or modified services involving information technology has meant that this category of guide has become increasingly important. As has already been indicated, an effective way of reaching the students is to reach the academic staff. Not only will these staff then be able to familiarise themselves with new developments (having also attended workshops?) and have the guides for reinforcement, but they will also (one hopes) pass on the newly found knowledge and skills to their students. Again the range of possible length and size of guide will depend on purpose, costs etc. Examples would be a one-page guide to the ECONLIT database, a twelve-page guide to the LEXIS/NEXIS online service, a twenty-page guide to printing and downloading from the library's databases (with coverage of each individual product), a guide to Internet resources which could equally come under the heading of Subject Guide

Institution-wide liaison

Opportunities to participate in externally-driven activities may present themselves in the institution. Equally, much important liaison work is carried out between the academic librarian and the central services. Both types of activity, although they may take a variety of forms, represent the librarian going 'over the wall' beyond the library's traditional boundaries. This journey into adjacent domains can provide definite benefits for all the constituents. Such activities:

- reinforce the perception of the library service as an integral part of the whole institution
- enhance the library's profile in terms of its centrality to the teaching and learning process
- make a valid contribution to the library's voice being heard
- provide opportunities to improve the credibility of the service
- offer a vehicle for reflecting on the delivery of services to users and their improvement
- offer opportunities for library staff development.

Externally-driven activities

All too often it is the Head of Library Services who alone from the library participates in institutional inspections, course/subject validation events, teaching quality assessments and quality audits, reviews etc. However, in the more enlightened organisations the culture may be more conducive to encouraging a high degree of participation by other members of library staff. At times this encouragement will run to involvement in external visits mainly from outside parties and also as part of teams validating/reviewing courses at associated institutions. Such involvement may include the library staff submitting reports on general services, services to departments or on teaching and learning activities. Some libraries produce a generic library profile or information pack which may be tailored to the needs of the department and/or the exercise in question. Library staff may be expected to take part in meetings or discussions which include issues wider than just those related to the library, for example assessment, teaching and learning methods, course monitoring and evaluation. These often provide good opportunities for staff to practice and develop certain transferable skills including:

- presentation skills
- negotiating skills
- skills of persuasion
- thinking 'on one's feet' and responding to often unexpected questions (these are not unheard of particularly in course validation events)
- constructing arguments calmly, coherently and convincingly.

Similarly, library staff may be called upon to form part of a team to visit other institutions for validation or other purposes. Again the opportunity for full participation is provided.

Involvement in these events is far from automatic. If the prevailing culture is one which is susceptible to new ideas, mature and confident in its staff, then the process of establishing precedents is more likely to run smoothly. A Head of Service who is receptive to this ethos will be eager to set the appropriate wheels turning.

Other Central Services

Liaison with other central services such as computing – in institutions where convergence has taken place this would be more straightforward – teaching and learning support units, careers and counselling services, centres for disabled students, reprographics departments and student union may form a vital part of academic library work. For example, the careers and library services both have an interest in the destination of students following courses of study including their employment prospects and the skills which they bring to the workplace, the types of professions into which they move or the postgraduate or research positions which they take up. They will also have a mutual interest in particular databases (particularly company information), provision of prospectuses, employment literature and other publications. The counselling and library services have common interests particularly in terms of study and information-handling skills and library tutorial support. All these services support each other in helping to provide a rounded educational and social experience to the student body.

These examples represent areas in which close cooperation and coordination often result in improvements to services. For example, it may be the case that current teaching of information-handling skills needs to be reviewed or updated. Much monitoring and evaluation work carried out by central services is helpful in identifying problems or inadequacies and, in collaboration with others, trying to rectify them.

There are many ways in which this cooperative approach may be fostered. Examples are:

- reciprocal visits to each of the services
- exchanges of guides, handouts and other literature
- shadowing or observing appropriate staff
- running jointly organised study skills workshops – either as part of a programme or as the need arises.

Conclusion

In this chapter we have tried to offer examples of the kinds of liaison activities which lead to academic integration but freely admit that comprehensive coverage is practically impossible. Inevitably there remain other areas which could provide fruitful opportunities. For example, in the process of recruitment and selection of certain library posts it is recommended that departmental representatives are involved in specifications, shortlisting of candidates and interviewing. Similarly, where staff appraisal systems operate, the inclusion of appropriate academic staff in providing feedback and comments into the process should be welcomed. Not only does this activity exemplify the collaborative spirit which the role of proactive librarian calls for, it also provides a vehicle for discussing, developing and evaluating academic integration in a structured way. It may also succeed in averting the danger of isolated thinking which is an accusation levelled at some academic libraries.

It is good practice to involve the departmental staff in as many activities as seems appropriate. The librarian should continually be seeking the views of the academic staff on the liaison activities so that improvements or modifications may be made. Evaluation does not always require structured and formal procedures. Informal discussions can be very helpful. The major objective of these activities is to foster a culture of partnership, cooperation and collaboration which results in an effective relationship that will ultimately benefit both the library and the academic community.

References

1. Veaner, A.B. 1985 to 1995: the next decade in academic librarianship, Part 2. *College and Research Libraries*, 46(4), 1985, pp.295–319.

2. Joint Funding Councils' Libraries Review Group. *Report*. Bristol: Higher Education Funding Council for England, 1993. (Follett Report)

3. Fielden, J. *Supporting expansion: a report on human resource management in academic libraries for the Joint Funding Councils' Libraries Review Group.* Bristol: Higher Education Funding Council for England, 1993. (Fielden Report)

4. Horton, J.J. Library liaison with social scientists: relationships in a university context. *Aslib Proceedings*, 29(4), 1977 pp.146–157.

5. Holbrook, A. The subject librarian and social scientists: liaison in a university setting. *Aslib Proceedings,* 36(6), 1984, pp.269–275.

6. Miller, L. Liaison work in the academic library. *RQ,* 16(3), 1977, pp.213–215.

7. Schloman, B.F. Lilly, R.S, Hu, W. Targeting liaison activities. *RQ,* 28(4), 1989, pp.496–505.

8. Divay, G. Ducas, A.M, Michaud-Oystryk, N. Faculty perceptions of librarians at the University of Manitoba. *College Research Libraries*, 48(1), 1987, pp.27-35.

9. Quiney, L. Social sciences, business, management and law. In Fletcher, J. *ed. Reader services in polytechnic libraries.* Aldershot: Gower, 1985, pp.62–94.

10. Atkinson, J. The image of the academic librarian *in* Harris, C. ed. *The new university library – issues for the 90s and beyond: essays in honour of Ian Rogerson.* London: Taylor Graham, 1994, pp.89-100.

3. Teaching and Learning

'I hear, and I forget
I see, and I remember
I do, and I understand'
Confucius

The importance of user education

Can we please finally dispense with the question of whether academic librarians should be anything other than totally involved in and committed to user education in post-compulsory education? It should form an integral part of the job description alongside collection development responsibilities, provision of reference and enquiry services, current awareness services and the rest. Only staff who have the appropriate skills should be appointed. If this particular element of the librarian's portfolio is to be taken seriously, these skills have to be made essential rather than just desirable. Academic librarians in the USA have no such hang-ups. Not only is user education built into the culture of the academic community but also it has a solid infrastructure across the country in terms of conferences, clearing houses and bulletin boards.

After providing an introduction and rationale, the purpose of this chapter is to put forward a model of academic user education which may be taken up and adapted for a variety of teaching and learning situations. This model may be viewed as a framework on which to hang a host of activities through which the academic community can become more proficient users of information. It is important that the day-to-day teaching and learning is based on a firm foundation of proven theory and informed good practice.

To include comprehensive coverage of this huge area would be impossible in a chapter such as this. We have therefore focused on activities which we have found to be effective, together with further reading where appropriate. Library and information support for individuals is covered in detail in Chapter 4.

Terminology

Some of the problems which are inherent in user education are reflected in the terminology. Below is a list of terms some of which have been fashionable in the past and others which are currently in use:

- user education
- bibliographic instruction
- library instruction
- reader instruction
- library skills
- information skills
- LIS (library and information) skills
- information-handling skills
- library orientation
- user orientation
- learner support
- tailored navigational support
- (part of wider) study skills.

A cursory glance down this list will identify certain differences of emphasis and even some points of tension. First, there is a dilemma between the short term (library skills) and the long term (user education). This is elaborated upon later. Second, there is the teaching (library instruction) and the learning (learner support). Third, there is the person (reader instruction) and the material (bibliographic instruction).

Our adoption of **user education** as the preferred term is based on the view that it represents more accurately the important elements of the activity – the user and education. It is *how* the user behaves and reacts in relation to information (regardless of format or environment) which represents the major emphasis. This happens to coincide with the current emphasis on the consumer or customer. Education reflects the view that, where possible, the knowledge and principles – internalised by skills practice – acquired should be capable of transfer into other simultaneous and subsequent environments. The aim of user education is therefore:

> *to enable students to become confident and self-reliant in both*
> *their current and future use of information and library services*
> *through mainly structured and formal group activities.*

Why the need for user education?

'Making the familiar strange'[1] has been adapted in other educational arenas as a useful device for highlighting and throwing into relief certain taken-for-granted everyday assumptions. The 'familiar' in this current scenario is represented by the library which runs an effective user education programme in tandem with the academic departments. The 'strange' is represented by the absence of such a programme. What would be the consequences of this?

- intolerable pressure on individual library staff at enquiry and issue desks?
- reliance on browsing and serendipity?
- lack of systematic, logical and realistic search strategies?
- uninformed students using the services – if at all – at the most basic level?
- anxious frightened students feeling isolated and marginalised by another support service?
- little prospect of the students acquiring short term or long term skills?
- increasing likelihood that students will become over-dependent on other people to provide their information needs?
- lower standards in assignments, examinations etc.?
- increasing likelihood of students having underdeveloped transferable skills such as IT-literacy skills or evaluative and critical skills?

Such a situation would of course be intolerable. The user-centred approach adopted in most post-compulsory education means ensuring, as far as possible, that individuals acquire the appropriate skills for independent study. Such a policy needs to be in harmony with the institution's teaching and learning strategy. The number of students who are currently involved in or entering further and higher education is so high that a group approach to user education is the only realistic option. While it certainly makes sense in terms of efficiency, the effectiveness of these programmes depends on a number of variables which are covered later in the chapter. The group approach would require the support of individual tutorials, demonstrations and enquiry services whenever possible.

Technology never stands still. There is enormous pressure on library and information services to make available the latest piece of electronic wizardry which will   supposedly propel the book and the librarian into obsolescence yet again! These developments have to be dovetailed into those of the parent institution and the library, understood by the academic and library staff and, finally, distilled and possibly repackaged for the student body. Two of the aims of user education programmes must surely be to enable students to feel comfortable with and undaunted by these developments and, secondly, to try to bring as many students as possible up to a common level of IT competence. Examples of developments which are currently exercising the minds of academic library and computing staff include electronic document delivery, electronic publishing, a variety of multi-media advances, networking and SuperJANET.

The electronic jungle thus created leads on to a further reason for user education: the growing complexity of information formats. For the foreseeable future it is an irony that the status quo is represented by continuous change. Even though technological development carries on apace the traditional information sources still remain. In varying degrees collections of monographs and periodicals form the backbone of many college and university library services – for teaching and research purposes. With some libraries stubbornly holding on to card catalogues together with the retention of material in microform and audiovisual formats, the spectrum with the 'traditional' signpost at the one end and 'postmodern' at the other is a fairly long one. It is through user education that this complex and potentially confusing picture can be explained and demonstrated to the academic community so that the whole range may be used to its full potential.

Those librarians who are converts to the 'education' element of user education realise the problems associated with short-term and long-term objectives. We have termed these approaches *restricted* and *elaborated*. It is worthwhile dwelling on the differences between them since the approach adopted in user education programmes will depend upon the institutional or library view regarding transferable skills. Table 3.1 shows the characteristics present in both.

Restricted	Elaborated
• short term	• long term
• library literacy	• information literacy
• course-oriented	• post course-oriented
• one library	• many libraries
• pragmatic	• conceptual
• emphasis on tools	• emphasis on strategy
• institution-oriented	• life-oriented

Table 3.1 Transferable skills: restricted versus elaborated approaches

Whilst these approaches are not meant to be mutually exclusive, librarians embarking on a programme of user education need to be clear where their emphasis lies. A certain proportion of the student body will make the jump from restricted to elaborated approaches without the assistance and proactivity of library staff. Of course, some students may already have some of the skills and understand the concepts which sit in the elaborated list – perhaps through previous educational opportunities or as a result of social upbringing. This will depend very much on the individual learner. In most cases such a jump has to be:

- part of an institutional ethos
- made explicit
- actively worked at
- reinforced with examples and practice.

Some skills will belong in both categories, for example keyboarding and use of material in different formats. Table 3.2 shows some typical practical examples of restricted and elaborated approaches to four areas within library and information work.

The model which is put forward is intended to be applied regardless of the approach. It becomes a matter of the librarian's judgement of balance and emphasis.

Skill category	Restricted	Elaborated
Retrieving information	How to carry out a search on CD-ROM	How to formulate a search strategy
Evaluating information	How to evaluate books, periodical articles & other sources	How to apply critical, evaluative and interpretative skills to information
Organising information	How to take notes from material & set up personal index for project	How to organise information for project management or research
Communicating information	How to write abstracts & record references	How to contribute to reports in a scholarly and consistent way

Table 3.2 Transferable skills:examples

User education: the practicalities

The framework on which this section is based is shown in Figure 3.1. Clearly not all the elements will carry the same importance; indeed, some elements may be excluded altogether. For this framework to provide practical help, it should be adapted to the requirements of individual library services – from the single hastily arranged teaching session to the five-part research skills module. The linear movement through the cycle is a conventional one:

- find out the needs of the target group
- establish the aims and objectives of the programme to meet those needs
- draw up the content of the programme and its individual units, together with the organisation of support and choice of methods
- deliver programme
- evaluate programme
- modify programme.

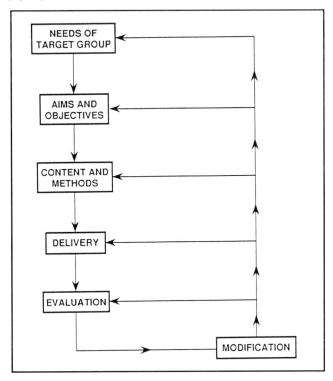

Figure 3.1 User Education: A Framework

User needs

The 1990s remains the decade of the consumer/customer. Early in the 1980s the importance of the consumer was a trend that accelerated through charterism, league tables, growing insistence on value for money and the gradual decline of deference. Meeting the needs of the user is therefore high on the academic library's priority list – and many would argue always has been. There is a variety of means whereby the library can find out the needs of the users and plan to meet them through programmes of user education.

Formal course monitoring and evaluation
Whether administered by the library or the parent institution, this feedback channel can provide valuable details of problem areas as perceived by the students, for example an inability to find material may reflect ignorance of catalogues, databases, classification systems, physical layout or perhaps a lack of creativity in library usage.

Informal feedback
This may take the form of comments made at enquiry and reference points, issue desks, during tutorials, via suggestions books. If possible, it is advisable to pool these suggestions and comments through one person as a filter so that trends may be established. An example would be the need for a series of workshops covering a particular database which was being accessed by users from a number of different departments.

Informal departmental feedback
Comments and observations may be made at a variety of liaison meetings such as those mentioned in the previous chapter. These may come from students or academic staff. Judging whether student comments are representative of larger groups is often a problem. The academic staff may notice trends arising out of assignments, projects or examinations. Poor quality of periodical citations by a particular group may indicate a need to provide guidance on searching for this type of literature.

Student group profiles
Depending on the detail already in the librarian's possession, it may be fruitful to build up profiles including:

- numbers on courses or modules
- modes of attendance
- types of assignments.

More in-depth detail may be obtained via questionnaires for example previous experience of libraries, whether direct from school, college or mature students and skills already acquired.

Questionnaires
Although surveys may provide valuable details about information needs, care should be taken over questionnaire fatigue and the resulting inadequate response rates. Naive questioning will usually result in affirmative responses, for example, 'Would an information skills workshop covering XYZ be useful to you?'

Evaluation of existing user education programmes
Evaluation, however brief and informal, sometimes throws up other areas in which students require further assistance. Separate sessions may then be arranged as appropriate. Evaluation is covered at the end of this chapter.

Observation
Merely watching library users' behaviour can be instructive. Users who may be wandering around fairly aimlessly, others who are patently experiencing problems using OPACs or other databases, may be accurate indicators of gaps in provision. Once the user group has been identified, steps may be taken to provide an appropriate session arranged either directly with the group or via the academic staff.

Course requirement
For some courses needs may have already been identified and built into the structure – perhaps with the librarian providing the initial input. An example taken from a Social Sciences undergraduate course involves the students constructing a short research proposal based on a literature search. A suitable user education programme is run and assessed jointly by library and academic staff.

These practical suggestions, particularly the formal ones, may represent a structured needs analysis to put before the management or resource holders. It is increasingly difficult to obtain any extra resources therefore evidence to support such requests is vital.

Aims and objectives

It is tempting to ignore the stage between assessing the needs of a target group and delivering the programme or unit. Although the literature covering instructional objectives is fairly extensive, a high level of complexity is unnecessary for most programmes. The reasons for explicitly stating aims and objectives can be many:

- they translate the target group's actual rather than perceived needs into concrete goals

- they provide a structure or framework on which to hang the programme and which benefits both librarian and students

- they help to articulate the programme for the academic departments or resource providers

- they provide benchmarks against which to measure or evaluate the programme's outcome.

Aims or goals tend to represent general statements of intent whilst objectives are specific measurable results that are required for the programme or unit's success. Table 3.3 shows an example of a first year undergraduate programme, with the overall aim and specific objectives for individual units.

Aims

To become familiar with the basic library services and facilities including a variety of materials in order to satisfy information needs within the first year. Topics to include orientation, use of library catalogues, periodicals and statistical sources.

Objectives

1. To FIND their way around the library through completion of a workbook.

2. To RETRIEVE all items on a reading list and, where necessary, IDEN-TIFY alternative titles.

3. To COMPILE a bibliography of twelve items using a recognised referencing system, together with the sources used to locate them.

4. To COMPARE six specific statistical sources outlining any important differences.

Table 3.3 Aims and objectives: examples

It is important to ensure that objectives are realistic and take into account availability of staff time as well as the level of success anticipated. They should also be appropriate given the needs of the group. Each of these elements has implications for the relevance and retention of the programme as well as the motivation of the participants.

When writing objectives, the verbs invariably denote ACTION. Examples would include:

Write	List	Explain
Find	Recall	Evaluate
Identify	Compare	Analyse
Differentiate	Complete	Summarise
Retrieve	Select	Assess
Construct	State	Give examples of
Compile	Describe	Demonstrate

Although they may be appropriate when writing general aims or goals, words or phrases such as the following are deemed too non-specific and unmeasurable:

- Know
- Be Interested In
- Be Aware Of
- Understand
- Obtain Working Knowledge Of
- Appreciate.

The task of finding out if the participants have accomplished what they set out to do will thus be that much easier. Whilst it is recognised as good educational practice to state clearly the purpose of any teaching/learning event, the level of detail remains dependent upon the professional judgement of the librarian.

The teaching and learning process

For convenience sake we have distinguished here between the teaching and learning process at two levels: the programme level and the unit level. Although there is a certain amount of interchangeability, we have attempted to concentrate on the practicalities of providing students with effective and enjoyable learning experiences. In particular, the criteria for an effective user education session are outlined and also the means by which these are translated in the learning environment regardless of the teaching methods. It has to be recognised, however, that there is a high degree of overlap between the criteria under which learning takes place, the content of the programme or unit, the methods used, the support provided and the skills and attitudes of the librarian. The library that has worked out the recipe and provides a balance across each of these variables has indeed developed a highly marketable product.

In this age of acronyms it may be considered helpful to use some mnemonics so that the essence of the teaching and learning criteria may be more easily captured and remembered.

R*I*T*A

This first mnemonic — at the level of the programme – reflects four ingredients whose application to a programme will provide a firm foundation for success:

- relevance
- integration
- timing
- assessability.

Relevance

Library skills are a means to an end although some librarians seem to act as if they were ends in themselves. For library users a user education programme has to demonstrate that it will help them to achieve their objectives — short or long term. If it is their perception that such a programme will not help, then they will either vote with their feet or take some convincing that the contrary is the case. On the other hand if the students recognise that the programme is *relevant* to their course needs, then they will be motivated and consequently more receptive to the learning opportunities offered.

One of the problems connected with relevance is communication. It may be the case that the relevance of the programme is lost on the targeted group – either through lack of explanation or misunderstandings. If the needs of the group have been identified in one of the ways outlined earlier in this chapter, the chances of providing a programme which is perceived as irrelevant should be minimised.

- Ensure that each element of the programme is firmly based on specific needs and subsequent objectives

- avoid the inclusion of a component which, although desirable, is only peripheral to the user group's needs

- do not sacrifice relevance for completeness. Often librarians try to include as much as possible in programmes since time tends to be at a premium. This should be resisted

- guides to user education programmes, course handbooks and general library literature should make explicit the links between the needs of the students and the relevance of the programmes

- inform students as to *why* they need to know about the topic. This helps to predispose them to learning.

Integration

Received wisdom suggests that course-related or course-integrated user education has the best chance of success. Library programmes which sit outside the students' courses of study may be perceived – understandably, some would say – as peripheral to requirements. However much encouragement is given by library and academic staff, voluntary workshops or other 'bolt on' sessions are at times seen as non-essential. Such perceptions go to the heart of the whole user education debate – the relationship between the library service and the academic departments. The librarians of an institution that places a high priority on the activities outlined in the previous chapter will find that integrated programmes will be more easily planned and more successfully delivered. Similarly, in educational institutions where particular emphasis is placed on the centrality of the library service to the teaching and learning process, integration of library activity into programmes of study becomes an accepted pattern. Although some including Malley [2] and Fleming [3] have commented on the continuum along which the various types of user education gravitate, the tightness of fit between academic department and library is a matter of professional judgement and cooperation. The precise terminological nuances of course-related versus course-integrated programmes are less important. Of greater importance is the creation of an environment in which the comfortability of academic librarians with their active participation in the teaching and learning process and the receptivity of the academic staff are enhanced. Figure 3.2 shows the notional stages between a good departmental-library relationship and the effective use of library services through user education.

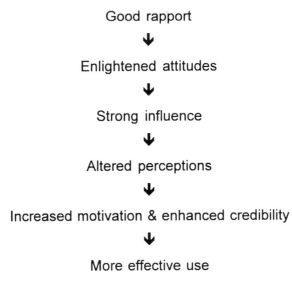

Good rapport

↓

Enlightened attitudes

↓

Strong influence

↓

Altered perceptions

↓

Increased motivation & enhanced credibility

↓

More effective use

Figure 3.2 Department-library relationship: stages

There are a number of practical ways which will help improve the likelihood of achieving an integrated programme:

- explore the department's current portfolio of courses looking for suitable vehicles for inclusion of a user education programme. Some lend themselves to the task more easily than others. For example, the more obvious possibilities would be communication skills or other study skills courses, research or project-based courses, assignments that require skills in using a range of electronic sources, subject-related areas such as law reports, company information, book reviews etc.

- ensure participation in course development so that library programmes may be included at an early stage

- adopt an incremental – or 'foot-in-the-door' – approach. Attempting to do too much too soon can be a problem, particularly for academic librarians new to a post. Concentrating efforts on a specific module or member of academic staff may be more fruitful than trying to be too ambitious. News of success which has been achieved from small beginnings will spread to other courses and staff

- be prepared to spend considerable time not only delivering the programmes themselves but also in laying the foundations for, preparing and evaluating them

- ensure that the library management is prepared to accept the time and effort

- encourage, where appropriate, the coordination of user education programmes and their integration – perhaps through the library's management structure. This provides uniformity of approach, strength in numbers, demonstration of priority or importance and financial support.

- discuss the possibility of collaborative teaching ventures such as joint or team teaching and peer observation. These may assist with credibility and coherence.

Timing

For learning to take place a number of elements have to coincide. One of these elements has to be good timing. The librarian's familiarity with the contents of the taught courses helps to pinpoint appropriate times to provide user education. For example, a programme of three units covering dissertation preparation and information retrieval in a taught Masters degree course is best organised for the period during which students are reflecting on suitable topics. A series of database workshops is unlikely to be well attended unless timed to coincide with specific course-related tasks. If the level of integration reflects the approaches adopted in the previous section, the programme will tend to be timed appropriately.

- Ensure, where possible, that the programme is timetabled alongside the other taught elements

- although often out of the librarian's control, there are certain times during the week when non-attendance at lectures and seminars is more prevalent – whether library-related or not. For undergraduates these are generally early morning, late afternoon and Friday afternoon in particular. The increase in student numbers, the resultant pressure on accommodation and the lengthening of the teaching day suggest that students have to accept such 'inconveniences'. This situation highlights the importance of using other means to facilitate student attendance, such as high levels of integration, relevance, credibility and motivation.

- be prepared to negotiate the timing of particular programmes. It may be necessary to fight your corner rather than be content with the times which the department has decided to give up. A series of units scheduled for Wednesday afternoons – sports afternoon and a favourite time for staff meetings – would be less than helpful

- repeat sessions, where necessary, for reinforcement or refreshment purposes.

Assessability

Nowadays one hears the phrase 'assignment-driven' being bandied about in higher education although it could apply equally to other sectors of education. We have a variety of outside agencies devoted to assessing education services – OFSTED, HEQC, HEFCE, FEFC together with other performance-related processes such as research assessment exercises and league tables. Within institutions themselves the importance of assessment is brought home to students in a variety of ways: assessment criteria are explicitly stated in course documentation; institutions are continually striving to find a more diverse range of assessment techniques; in modular programmes students are often heavily influenced in their option choices by assessment methods. It is then hardly surprising that assessment should act as one force in motivating students to action. The main benefit of direct assessment of user education programmes is that it succeeds in focusing student attention on the programme itself. Long-term benefits are, however, more difficult to gauge. Some would argue that assessability is a spurious reason for inclusion in a programme. One major downside of assessment is the workload that inevitably accompanies it. Library and information skills may also be assessed by academic tutors as part of some broader subject-related assignment, for example 20% of an assignment could be devoted to bibliography construction.

- ensure that any course documentation states clearly the assessment criteria for library and information activities.

- become familiar with the assessment techniques applied to the courses to which the user education programmes are related

- request that completed exercises be handed in to the librarian or tutor. This helps to gauge students' skills and the success of the user education programme and it also acts as a motivator.

F*A*R*M*U*S*I*C

This second mnemonic – at the level of the unit or single session – represents a collection of variables which, when present in one unit, will increase the likelihood of substantial learning taking place:

- feedback

- activity

- reinforcement

- motivation

- understanding

- structure

- interaction

- clarity

The degree to which each is present in a particular unit will vary. For example, the lecture (or talk, explanation) about the publications cycle may contain a tight structure, be a model of clarity but lack opportunities for activity and feedback. Likewise, an exploration of business information sources within a small group may provide activity, interaction between students and library staff as well as building upon previous knowledge and understanding. It may, however, lack a way of reinforcing the learning. Methods of teaching and learning will be explored later in the chapter.

Feedback

Feedback from teacher to learner needs to be positive and constructive so that the receiver becomes motivated to learn more. Praise acts as a great motivator. Put downs produce negative feelings which are not conducive to effective learning. Feedback is given most appropriately in more active learning situations, for example group work, seminars supported by self-study or workbooks. A workshop which provides a group of students with hands-on experience of a set of databases would require the librarian to give extensive feedback on participants' rate of progress and performance generally. Such gentle constructive encouragement can instil confidence in students who may be daunted or overawed by the educational or technological environment.

Activity

Research suggests that the quotation at the head of this chapter contains more than a modicum of truth. Student learning is enhanced by a relevant activity. Such activities may take a variety of forms such as group exercises, individual exercises followed by comparison and discussion or use of databases and networks within the library. Although the nature of the user education unit may not lend itself to active learning, it is recommended that all avenues are exhausted in the search. Often an activity may be incorporated into a unit in order to break it up. Attention spans – and not just of students – tend to be fairly short and one method of overcoming this is to provide a diversity of activities. However, a large number of activities can have a counterproductive learning effect in the same way as only one activity spread over a long period. A balance needs to be struck.

Reinforcement

Practice makes perfect; it also helps to reinforce learning. A demonstration of a CD-ROM database has a more beneficial effect if students are given the opportunity to practice and develop the skills and techniques shown. A written guide to the library's OPAC is a useful tool for students but its usefulness will be enhanced if the students spend some time practising the procedures. Other methods of reinforcement include:

- repeating certain important points of explanation for emphasis
- explaining a phenomenon from two or three different perspectives
- using a variety of teaching and learning methods in one unit
- using a variety of learning supports such as OHTs, flipcharts and handouts
- summarising frequently and getting others to do so
- making use of examples, anecdotes and analogies

Students need the freedom to make mistakes and learn from them preferably in a non-threatening environment.

Motivation

Over the years many texts have been written on this complex psychological phenomenon. Each individual is motivated by a unique set of variables. In any user education unit effective learning will take place when the motivation levels of teachers and learners are at their highest. So how can these levels be achieved?

The *learner* is more likely to be motivated if:

- the unit is relevant and well-timed
- the unit includes a diversity of content and method
- the content is of interest to the learner
- the learning environment is comfortable
- the unit avoids information overload
- the unit has a clear structure

- the librarian shows enthusiasm for the subject
- the unit is assessable
- academic staff are present or participate in the learning process

The *librarian* is more likely to be motivated if:

- the learners show interest and enthusiasm
- the learners participate and ask questions
- an innovative or unusual teaching/learning method is adopted
- the learning environment is comfortable
- the work of the unit has been suitably prepared

Motivation can be a powerful emotion and is the key to the learning process. Unless both parties are highly motivated, the effect of the other seven elements will be limited accordingly.

Understanding

Under this umbrella may be found a variety of mental activities which are happening subconsciously. The activities include:

- building on existing knowledge and skills
- digesting information, i.e. sorting out the important parts and discarding the unimportant
- internalising the information or establishing a sense of ownership.

Ideally understanding requires continuity from unit to unit so that progression can take place. Often librarians do not have this continuity at their disposal or, if they do, individual units are separated by weeks or even months.

Although this is a difficult area about which to offer practical advice, certain background information will help the librarian to focus the unit:

- find out what user education the students have already received
- familiarise yourself with their course and its structure to find out what has already been covered
- discuss with appropriate tutors the strengths and weaknesses of the group in terms of study skills
- gain an overview of existing knowledge levels by asking questions at the start of a user education unit. For example, 'how many of you have used a CD-ROM before?', 'how familiar are you with XYZ printed index'? etc.

This need not be a detailed exercise but rather a way of knowing at what level to pitch the current unit. There is unlikely to be a balanced knowledge/skills base across the group

- continue to ask questions periodically throughout the session to try and gauge level of understanding
- explain the context and background to the content
- allow specific times during the session when students are able to reflect on the content. If the pace of the unit is too fast, the process of digesting the new information becomes problematic
- explain the reasons for doing a particular exercise or learning a particular technique. It is sometimes necessary to make explicit the connections between existing and new knowledge
- use examples and anecdotes that are related to students' prior experience and classes.

Structure

A structure is a 'set of interconnecting parts of any complex thing' (*Concise Oxford Dictionary*). People learn best when the material to be learned has a recognised and logical structure. Often it is referred to as a framework on which to hang knowledge and skills. In the absence of an explicit structure students will invariably strive to provide their own since people generally have a strong motivation to order things logically (even non-librarians!). Depending on the complexity of the content and the connections between its various parts, this structuring will require students to divert their attention from the material to be learned. The structuring – whether in words, handout, OHT, flipchart or board – will leave students to concentrate on making sense of the material itself. Often the structure of a unit reflects the objectives explicitly stated. A structure may be viewed as a series of mental paragraphs which divide the contents into digestible chunks. This notion has already been alluded to in the previous sections on motivation and understanding.

- Have a beginning, a middle and an end
- make the structure explicit
- make a point of closing, reviewing and summing up each segment of the structure
- tell the students what they are to learn, provide the learning experience and tell the students what they (should) have learned
- make space between segments.

Interaction

This variable represents a combination of the contents of some of the others. It can include:

- activity – although this can be carried out by one individual
- feedback – although this is from librarian to learner
- asking questions – part of ascertaining understanding
- getting students to summarise – part of reinforcement.

The underlying thread of these disparate elements is that of active learning through dialogue and collaboration.

Clarity

Clarity may be applied in a variety of user education perspectives:

- clarity of thought, for example in preparing objectives.
- clarity of structure.
- clarity of expression and explanation.
- clarity of support material.

Many students find certain aspects of libraries complex and certainly,, the diversity of available formats, IT-related services, loan periods, different staffing functions etc. can be confusing. It is therefore vital that clarity is sought regardless of the content of the unit and the methods used:

- make a point of checking content for jargon or other technical language which may provoke the ubiquitous 'glazed' look. Each profession has its own jargon but what is second nature to librarians may be confusing or unintelligible to the uninitiated

- ask questions to test clarity

- pilot user education units on a colleague or other appropriate person(s) for clarity of expression including written material

- ensure that any graphical representations are clear visually and conceptually. One reason for using such images is to clarify complexity!

Teaching and learning methods

Constraints

At times librarians can feel under pressure when participating in user education. This is particularly so if the units do not form part of a continuous programme. The pressure to achieve objectives within a limited time period may be enormous. It is therefore vital to ensure that only the core content is included and that the temptation to overload the session is resisted. When it comes to learning, less means more! This focus on the need for impact highlights the importance of teaching and learning methods and the part they play in maximising student learning.

There are several possible influences on the choice of specific methods.

Staffing levels

Some libraries are more generously staffed than others. Also there may be insufficient time allocated to user education in relation to other duties. Besides team teaching certain other methods may require more than one member of staff to function effectively, e.g. workshops, certain group activities. A significant constraint may lie in the underdeveloped or inappropriate skills of the librarian(s).

Size of groups

This criterion can have a decisive effect on the type of unit planned. Libraries have little control over the total recruitment of students to institutions which are under pressure from central government to fulfil target intakes in the climate of a declining unit of resource. In the ideal world and with a close relationship between academic departments and library the group sizes would be determined by the purpose of the programme. Taking an extreme case, a lecture theatre seating 250 would be inappropriate for acquiring the skills of database searching – although we have seen this done through the use of OHTs! Negotiation of group size can be a delicate affair. On the one hand the librarian may take up an assertive position of knowing the optimum number for the planned unit but also recognises the realistic situation in terms of timetables, accommodation and course structure. Does the librarian hold out for the ideal (and possibly lose out completely), accept the situation as given (inadequate though it is and likely to become the norm) or negotiate a compromise?

Time available

The librarian who has only one hour in which to help prepare students for project or dissertation work is likely to approach the task differently from a colleague who has one whole day. Increasingly, the availability of time for devotion to user education represents a continuing dialogue between departments and library. Gaining more time relieves the pressure to cram existing sessions and provides opportunities for the use of a greater variety of teaching methods. However, the pressure may then be transferred to the librarian's wider role or, indeed, to colleagues. Are there enough hours to carry out extended user education programmes alongside the other duties? Which brings us back to staffing levels and organisational priorities.

Facilities

How often are user education programmes influenced by the physical environment and facilities available to library staff? The decision about the location of programmes is often determined by practicalities or indeed made elsewhere.

Library accommodation:
- may have limited space and/or teaching rooms
- may have purpose-built computer labs, training suite etc
- should provide a comfortable familiar environment for the librarian.
- may provide an uncomfortable environment for users
- has the material at hand for activities
- may have other librarians eager to use the same space or facilities at the same times, especially at peak times during the year.

Departmental accommodation:
- may be difficult to book due to pressure from other departments
- may provide credibility for the programme. Being located in their backyard the programme is more likely to be perceived as part of the academic package rather than being bolted on
- may provide the librarian with unfamiliar territory
- may give rise to problems of demonstrating library material although portability of material or students may be possible.

Combinations

Before considering the practicalities of particular teaching and learning methods, the desirability of combining different ones in each session needs to be highlighted. It is recognised that no one specific method is suitable for all occasions and that a variety of approaches positively assists the learning process. Fig. 3.3 shows an example of a dissertation preparation day for final year undergraduates incorporating a diversity of methods.

Whatever methods are adopted the FARMUSIC variables need to be considered and applied appropriately in each session.

A useful technique for mapping user education sessions is to provide a grid on which to pictorialise the combination of methods used. Fig 3.4 shows an example of such a grid for a one and a half hour CD-ROM workshop/demonstration together with a skeleton of the content.

Time	Activity	Method
9.00 - 9.30	Aims and objectives	Talk, exercise
9.30 - 10.00	Introduction to the literature	Talk
10.00 - 10.30	Defining research proposal	Exercise
10.30 - 11.00	Coffee	
11.00 - 11.30	Search methods	Video
11.30 - 1.00	Sources: printed and electronic	Discussion, demonstration, exercises
1.00 - 2.00	Lunch	
2.00 - 2.30	Feedback from exercises	Discussion
2.30 - 3.00	Citing references, etc.	Talk, exercise
3.00 - 3.15	Tea	
3.15 - 3.45	Interlibrary loans and other document delivery	Talk, demonstration
3.45 - 4.30	What is expected? Examples of past dissertations	Discussion
4.30 - 5.00	Review and evaluation	Discussion

Figure 3.3 Searching The Literature

Content

- introduction (aims, what is a CD-ROM, pros/cons of format)
- demonstration of specific database
- search using a student's example
- discussion of the planning, search strategy etc
- exercise on networked PCs
- feedback on progress, problems
- use of CD-ROMs relative to other formats.

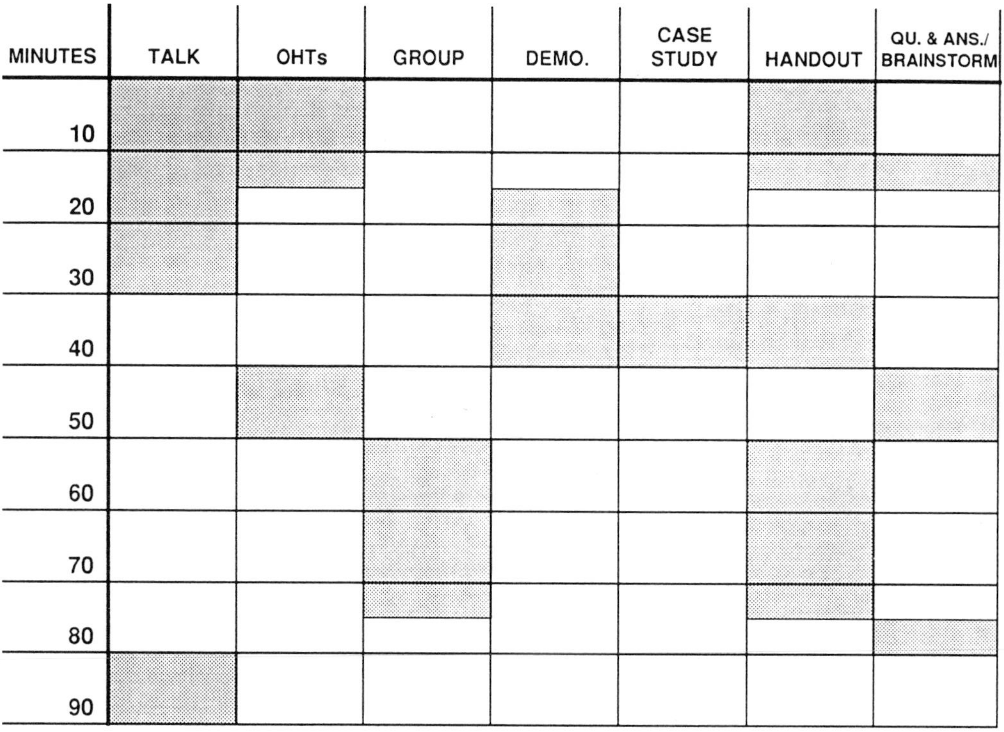

MINUTES	TALK	OHTs	GROUP	DEMO.	CASE STUDY	HANDOUT	QU. & ANS./ BRAINSTORM
10	■	■				■	
20	■	■		■		■	■
30	■			■			
40				■			
50		■					■
60			■			■	
70			■			■	
80			■			■	■
90	■						

Figure 3.4 Grid technique: a CD-ROM demonstration

The grid assists also in the planning of the session as well as checking that it has a balance across the methods. Just as it is inadvisable to stick to one method throughout, it can be counterproductive to allow the session to be fragmented by too many different approaches. Experience will tell whether a balance has been struck although each group will react or behave differently depending on other variables, for instance group make-up, dynamics, physical environment, time of day and so on.

Specific methods

There is a huge number of texts currently on the market that provide theoretical underpinning of and practical advice on teaching and learning methods in further and higher education. A selection of those particularly helpful to librarians is listed under further reading.

The main methods are listed under two categories: *lecture-based* and *group-based*.

Lecture-based

Examples include:

- formal lecture

- demonstration

- explanation

- informal talk

Group-based

Examples include:

- discussion

- buzz groups

- simulation

- case study

- seminar

- brain storming

- game

The above would generally be supported by the use of flipcharts, white/black boards, overhead transparencies (or equivalent software), handouts and other literature guides.

Many of the methods within these categories lend themselves to modification and alteration in order to suit the purpose of the session. Creative adoption of combinations, as mentioned previously, can be particularly effective. Since these two categories include the bulk of methods currently in use in the library environment, we have focused on them. A third category would include a miscellany of methods, each of which has its own distinctive qualities and problems. Because of their individual nature they are covered in the further reading. Examples of such methods would be supported self-study including workbooks, and open learning.

For each of the two categories practical hints are provided together with suggestions for variations to help motivation, maintain freshness and encourage risk taking.

Lecture-based

Practical hints
- possess the environment – be in the room *before* and *after* the students

- be enthusiastic about what you are saying and doing
- look at the audience and make eye contact with as many as possible
- structure the lecture to be heard rather than read
- move around to maintain visual variety
- use gestures or pauses for emphasis or impact
- vary the pace
- use appropriate examples or anecdotes to maintain interest
- aim for maximum impact at beginning and end
- be prepared to make a fool of yourself sooner or later and be prepared to laugh it off
- don't be afraid of silences – they encourage reflection
- students generally welcome authority and direction
- don't be afraid to make a mistake and admit it
- don't hide behind waffle – students invariably recognise it
- avoid inflexible statements from which you may later have to retreat
- check out room, equipment, seating arrangements, teaching aids, accessories, handouts, and other support material, signs for directions, windows, blinds, temperature, acoustics etc
- don't intimidate students into submission by a formal autocratic approach (to combat nerves?)
- make a conscious effort to speak more slowly than normal conversational mode
- inject some humour into the proceedings when appropriate and try to make it seem spontaneous – it helps sometimes to direct humour at oneself
- encourage a colleague to observe your teaching and vice-versa if students are disrupting or interrupting your flow; ask them to share their observations/comments with the rest
- students have more respect for the librarian who demonstrates control over unruly or problematic students.

Possible variations
- interact with your audience
- encourage questions

- repeat questions if necessary
- ask students to discuss a question in twos or threes
- split the lecture into clearly distinguished sections – the so-called sliced lecture – with different emphases, talkers, methods, media, pace and style
- try to limit sections to a maximum of fifteen minutes
- provide time for reading a handout, tackling a short test or digesting a new idea
- use demonstrations, concrete examples, specific situations or other props for illumination
- use activities common in smaller groups, e.g. buzz groups, brainstorming
- if the room allows, rearrange furniture and groupings, e.g. cocktail party or cafe-style models (standing or sitting in groups)
- ask questions of individuals, sections of the audience or clustered groups rather than asking into the ether
- create a participative atmosphere where interaction and dialogue may be expected and welcomed
- be aware of the possibility that participation will create noise or a buzz which may require assertiveness to close
- when injecting an activity into the talk, ensure that the participants know WHY they are doing it, WHAT they are expected to do, HOW they should go about it and WHEN they should finish
- don't be afraid to risk using a new method.

Group-based

Practical hints
- try to let the groups run themselves once divided up
- be prepared to facilitate possibly in conjunction with a colleague – library or academic staff
- encourage individuals to participate but be non-dominating and cooperative
- ensure furniture settings are appropriate for the purpose of the session including make-up and size of groups
- always keep in mind the objectives of the session since group work has a tendency to diversion

- ensure familiarity with accommodation, if not situated in the library
- allow plenty of preparation time
- praise, encourage and compliment whenever possible
- make use of boards, flipcharts etc. to review, summarise, illuminate and clarify group responses.

Possible variations

- experiment with seating and table arrangements
- provide variety by mixing group work in twos, threes and fours, together with swapping of individuals from group to group
- use brainstorming to break down group reserve and create links between librarian and individuals
- where a video or other audiovisual medium is part of the session, encourage students to create an agenda beforehand to focus the mind
- use exercises to be peer-assessed
- use icebreakers to break down group reserve and help group to gel more quickly.

Overhead transparencies and handouts

Traditionally each of these has succeeded in supporting formal user education sessions. OHTs or acetates are often the focus of student attention when they are ineffective for one reason or another. Their effective use can go unnoticed. The following advice on their usage has been gleaned from the literature and our experience and that of colleagues:

- ensure clearly written and structured OHTs
- ensure visibility from furthest point
- make diagrams and connections simple
- avoid clutter or overcrowding
- use lower case lettering for ease of viewing
- avoid elaborate fonts
- make available as handouts
- avoid excessive use within one session
- use colour where possible

- avoid list after list after list
- always try them out beforehand
- avoid overuse of 'progressive reveal' and overlay techniques
- avoid standing in front of screen and obscuring view
- use a pointer (pencil?) to indicate item on screen
- speak to the audience not to the screen
- turn off projector when not in use
- if audience is likely to copy from screen, ensure they are given enough time
- leave some gaps in the transparencies to be filled in during the session
- produce transparencies in similar house style
- ensure copies are kept on disc for future use or alterations.

There are a number of software packages currently on the market, such as Power Point, which represent a PC-based method of presenting information to groups. Whether traditional or electronic formats are adopted, professionally produced information reflects favourably on you and will enhance the credibility of the library and the parent institution.

The above point also applies to the design and production of support literature or handouts. These allow students to concentrate their minds on the issues without being diverted by note-taking or desperately trying to remember items. Here are some hints on handout usage:

- use printed OHTs as handouts and tell the students so – they may be re-duced, combined on a page and repackaged (with due regard to copyright restrictions)
- use interactive handouts (sometimes called 'active' or 'skeletal' handouts) with gaps to be filled in during the session (see Appendix II)
- issue lecture notes as a handout
- consider hole-punching for inclusion in binders.
- include plenty of white space – even in non-interactive handouts – for note-taking, results of brainstorms or discussions
- ensure high quality of production within the budgetary constraints.
- make use of headings, bold print, variety of fonts, graphical representation and logos

- ensure copies are kept on disc for future use or alterations. The question of the timing of handout distribution is a difficult one and depends on the nature and purpose of the session and the control of the librarian.

There are various options:

- distributing handouts at the very beginning. This may limit the rustle of paper and ensuing discussion to the initial settling-in period. On the other hand the students may be lulled into a passive mode in the belief that the handout is a substitute for participation. For the interactive handout this is the only real option

- distributing handouts during the session. This may have the disadvantage of breaking-up the flow of the session. However, this may be the intention! It may be an appropriate way of changing the session's direction or just providing a period of reflection

- distributing handouts after the session. If students know the timing they may be tempted to revert to passive mode. On the other hand they are able to concentrate on the content of the session in the knowledge that the hand-outs will reinforce their learning.

Computer-assisted user education

The adoption of the computer as a medium for teaching and learning has been attractive for a number of years. However, progress has been slow and spasmodic until recently. The increasing numbers of students and the more focused search for alternative teaching methods have provided some promising examples for library, information and wider study skills purposes.

A series of computer packages for use by library and information staff has been developed and thoroughly tested by the University of Glasgow [4]. Further details of the Teaching with Independent Learning Technologies (TILT) project can be found on the World Wide Web at the URL http://www.elec.gla.ac.uk/TILT/. The following elements of the project are currently available:

- how to choose books and journals

- library search skills (Business and general)

- computer sources

- study skills.

They have the advantages of flexibility and networkability so that they may be either incorporated into structured user education programmes or taken up by individual students and followed at their own pace. Their interactive nature provides feedback and advice. The content of the packages is deliberately generic to allow more widespread accessibility.

As students become more computer-literate, the attraction of this teaching method is likely to increase. However, a word of caution is required. Computer-assistance in learning requires for success a large proportion of the FARMUSIC criteria referred to above – as with any other method. For example, the high degree of interaction and feedback may have to be balanced against a lack of clarity or the problem of building on existing competences.

Support for user education

For the user education programmes of any library to be effective, it is crucial that they are well supported. What form should this support take? Inevitably, the kind of support received by each individual librarian will vary enormously – from the librarian working on his or her own initiative and nothing else to the subject librarian with the backing of a whole team of clerical and technical support together with a management team that supplies the resources, staff development and coordination required. Needless to say, the support of the academic staff is vital for success.

Managerial support

The librarian does not work in isolation. He or she works in the context of the institution of which the library represents one central service. The teaching and learning programmes and the user education programmes need to be working to the same ends. The political and financial support required for user education is likely to be more forthcoming in an integrated and mutually respected departmental structure. A difficult balancing act is sometimes performed within the library itself since there are a variety of stakeholders all competing for resources and other support. Financial resources – in terms of money, staff and equipment – which are deployed for user education are diverted from other equally essential parts of the service. This is the manager's constant dilemma. However, not only does it mean other parts receiving less but also the nature of successful user education programmes can have a considerable knock-on effect. Enquiry and reference services become busier; CD-ROM and networked databases are put under pressure; interlibrary loan and other document delivery services become overworked; printing and stationery budgets are pushed to the limit. The list could go on. Staff may have to be redeployed or extra staff brought in to cope with the increases. There may also be evidence of feelings of resentment amongst some library staff because of the (perceived) high profile and elitism which is at times accorded to this element of the library's role. Management support may be required for training and staff development to enhance or update teaching skills and for coordination of diverse programmes across different subjects, campuses, departments. Where the staffing structures and organisational culture are not conducive to such programmes, management support in initiating them is crucial. Such support can provide an important function within the institution in building alliances, demonstrating the library's value and highlighting achievements.

Administrative, technical and clerical support

This sometimes overlooked trio of supporting structures can make or break user education. Examples of clerical support include word processing and production of handouts, OHTs, lecture notes, signs and guiding. Administrative support may take the form of statistical logs (see Appendix III), room and furniture settings, checking of equipment and coordination of handout packages (see Appendix IV). Examples of technical support include troubleshooting in the use of database networks, liaison with computing and other internal media agencies, as well as outside agencies.

Peer Support

It is important that other library staff support user education not only in terms of goodwill to cope with knock-on effects but also in the sharing of ideas, good practice, experience and expertise. Peer support and review tend to be overlooked as strong influences on progress and development.

Evaluation

The problems inherent in the evaluation of user education programmes are reflected in the survey results within the UK further and higher education sectors. According to Morgan [5] evaluation of programmes was carried out by 40% of academic libraries. Lack of time, limited expertise, lack of motivation, the difficulties of measuring short- and long-term benefits as well as the balance between evaluation of the learning process and the learning outcomes – these have all been put forward as potential barriers to progress.

Why should we want to evaluate user education?

- to improve the mechanics of the programme (the learning process)
- to judge the appropriateness of the content
- to measure the benefits that accrue (the learning outcome)
- to provide accountability for library and institutional managers

The first category would answer questions such as:

- was the teaching room adequate in size and layout?
- was the length of the session suited to the purpose?

- did students participate when required?
- were group sizes right for the purpose?
- were presentation styles appropriate?
- were the teaching aids helpful?
- was the session's timing right?

The second category would answer questions such as:

- was the content pitched at the appropriate level?
- was coverage comprehensive or were there gaps?
- did students see the value of the content?
- did the session build upon knowledge or skills already acquired?

The third category would answer questions such as:

- did the students acquire the skills or knowledge which the session set out to provide?
- did the students' attitudes and behaviour change as a result of the session?

The fourth category would answer questions such as:

- is the programme efficient and cost-effective?
- does the programme provide the visibility or promotional purpose intended?
- is programme evaluation helpful in staff appraisal?
- is the programme helpful in terms of internal review or external quality assessment purposes?

The approach taken in this book is a realistic and pragmatic one: it is the 'rich picture' approach. By adopting a variety of methods and by viewing user education from different perspectives, a fuller picture is drawn. Although it may seem heretical, it is sound advice to avoid 'getting hung up' on formal methods of evaluation. Informal and subjective methods can still provide useful trends and patterns. The formal methods applied – directly or indirectly – by academic departments may be the most effective in measuring the achievement of objectives, for example through assignments, compilation of bibliographies, tests and exercises. Particularly valuable are assessment procedures built into integrated user education programmes.

Questionnaire

The questionnaire survey is the most commonly found method of evaluating user education (see Appendix V). The reasons for its popularity are:

- ease of completion
- good response rate (if administered directly after session)
- librarian's presence helps clarification
- anonymity.

It also has its disadvantages:

- immediate response leaves no time for reflection
- difficulty of constructing a 'foolproof' questionnaire
- difficulty of measuring attitudes.

Participants need to be aware of the programme's aims and objectives so that they may be able to judge their progress in achieving them. There is a danger that participants may make a judgement on objectives which they themselves have set and which may be at odds with those set by the organisers or instructors.

Formal discussion groups

Formal discussion groups consist of groups of students assembled specifically to air their views on a programme. They are sometimes called focus or feedback groups. The advantages of these groups are that:

- they may be integrated and timetabled into the programme
- the facilitator can be a member of the academic staff, a librarian or an independent person. In the latter case groups may respond more freely and honestly
- a semi-structured questionnaire may provide a basis for the discussion
- individuals are able to develop a collective group confidence.

The disadvantages of this method include:
- the potential for the inaccurate recording of views fed back
- the problem of unrepresentative nature of responses
- facilitation is a difficult skill to master
- the motivation of students to attend and participate in the review.

Informal discussion

The views of participants both during and after user education sessions can act as valuable indicators of success. The librarian inevitably builds up a picture during the session – through student attentiveness, facial expressions and other body language and questions and answers – of how well the unit is working. A participative dialogical approach helps in terms of accuracy. Informal impressionistic views expressed at the end of a session can be equally illuminating.

Interviews

One-to-one interviews (of the structured or semi-structured variety) tend to be used only rarely for evaluating teaching and learning programmes. The major constraints of the interview method are its time consuming and staff intensive nature. The benefits of interview are that:

- it is particularly effective in drawing out views and probing problem areas
- it may be used for providing evidence of knowledge acquired
- individuals who are intimidated or daunted by group discussions will give responses more readily
- it may be carried out in a structured, semi-structured or unstructured way depending on its purpose.

Tests and exercises

The use of tests is more widespread in academic libraries in the USA than the UK. In the former case they tend to be administered before and after user education programmes in order to measure the amount of learning that has taken place. In the UK exercises may be used more widely for reinforcing learning rather than for assessment purposes. Tests and exercises are usually straightforward to administer but their main drawback is that they only measure short-term retention of skills and knowledge which students may then fail to apply in different information-seeking situations, i.e. the skills have not been transferred. If individual exercises are marked, the extra work involved should not be underestimated.

Indirect assessment

A number of user education programmes, particularly those that have been integrated into more extensive taught courses, may be evaluated via student assignments, essays, seminars, presentations or bibliography compilations. Where assessment criteria are explicitly stated, students are generally more highly motivated to achieve success. The major problem with indirect assessment is one of cause and effect – the attribution of levels of achievement to specific information-related sessions. If assessment is carried out by academic staff, close cooperation is required to relate results to user education input.

The significance of other indirect evaluation exercises should not be underestimated. The departmental and institutional monitoring and evaluation of quality and standards will highlight problems associated with larger user education programmes. Successes are less frequently recognised. Single user education units are unlikely to be taken into consideration. The UK Funding Councils' Teaching Quality Assessment exercises are taking notice of efforts to evaluate the library generally and its teaching programmes in particular as indicators of quality. Details of numbers of students participating, types of programmes offered and numbers of hours involved are all helpful quantitative guides. Funding Council assessors have also been observing user education programmes as part of their visits. Such integrated evaluative vehicles help to build up a rich picture.

Conclusion

During the last twenty-five years much has been written in the professional literature about user education in all its guises. Many of the arguments put forward in the 1990s for developing the programmes themselves and the skills of the library staff who organise, administer, deliver and evaluate them, seem to us to be convincing. The imperative to become an ever more information-rich society necessitates that students develop and foster appropriate skills to help in their professional advancement. These and other transferable skills will provide competitive advantage in future career progression.

References

1. Delamont, S. All too familiar? a decade of classroom research. *Educational Analysis,*, 3(1) pp69 – 83.

2. Malley, I. *Basics of information skills teaching.* London: Clive Bingley, 1984.

3. Fleming, H. ed. *User education in academic libraries.* London: Library Association Publishing, 1990.

4. Creanor, L. *A hypertext approach to information skills: development and evaluation.* Glasgow: Teaching with Independent Learning Technologies (TILT), 1995.

5. Morgan, S. *Performance assessment in academic libraries.* London: Mansell, 1995.

4. Library support for the individual

'Our vision needs to remain on the individual user'[1]

Introduction

To provide a library service which takes proper account of the needs of individuals has always been important to the successful academic library. However, the state of flux in which the post-sixteen education sector finds itself means that this aim is becoming increasingly difficult to achieve. This Chapter and Chapter 5 (which addresses the specific services to non-traditional students) consider why the individual has become the main focus of the service. Both chapters examine particular services as examples of good practice.

The previous chapter covered the formal user education programmes aimed primarily at large groups. The success of these ventures depends on relevance, timing, integration and a host of other elements. But one element that will be required is support for the individual, perhaps not immediately but at certain points during the student's course. Point of need assistance forms an important back-up to teaching, learning and research.

Mass higher education

The massification of further and higher education has affected students and academic staff in a variety of ways. Most students are entering a new and alien world in which socialisation and orientation can be prolonged. There is a danger that individuality and identity become subsumed in this 'learning experience'. Some students never come to terms completely with these difficulties but adopt coping strategies which may not be conducive to effective learning. These strategies may be applied in their relationships with the library and the other support services. Students need reassurance and support so that they do not allow feelings of isolation to take the upper hand. Institutional counselling and pastoral support are however being placed under enormous pressure.

Academic staff

For individual academic staff the most significant effect of this sustained increase in student recruitment has been to erode their time. Consequently, there is less class contact with students. This reduction in formal teaching hours translates into student requests for discussions of assignments and meetings with groups concerning seminar presentations at other times. The workload of these staff – administration, assessment, monitoring and evaluation and pressure to complete research – has increased as a direct result of the expansion of higher education though with limited support from the government. Indeed, this strategy of increasing the input of students into further and higher education has been followed by the demand from government for the euphemistically termed 'efficiency gains'. The frustration of academic staff is both evident and understandable.

Student-centred learning

The most significant reason for concentrating attention on individual users revolves around the ubiquitous notion of a student-centred approach to learning. Both philosophical and practical difficulties arise out of this move. It is ironic that the educationally sound principles that aim to ensure that students learn self-reliance and independence also produce a knock-on effect by increasing demand for learner support. The more confident users of the library become, the greater are their expectations of the service provided. The greater choice which modularisation is providing, the increased emphasis on resource-based learning which courses demand, together with the increase in the number and variety of group activities have all put pressure on the library service and on the students themselves. The library has to modify its services and the way they are offered, with many students having to become accustomed to different ways of learning. The term coined by cynics to describe this pedagogical shift is the BOFOFY method (Buzz Off and Find Out For Yourself).

Although rather crudely put, there is a grain of truth in the underlying thinking. Student-centred learning is having the effect of pushing more and more students into the arms of the support services, mainly the library. As part of this approach to learning, students are expected to negotiate the complexities of the contemporary academic library. They have to familiarise themselves with traditional library procedures, such as classification schemes and complex loans and fines regimes. On top of this, however, users are confronted with a daunting plethora of IT-related services, some of which require generous amounts of individual support, particularly in the early stages. Self issue, renewal and reservation systems, open access and networked databases – with purportedly user-friendly interfaces and helpful graphics – and the general shift towards accessing information, appear daunting to new students, not to mention to some academic staff. Where individuals are undersupported in this sometimes 'hostile' technological environment, an unhealthy competitive climate may be created. This climate manifests itself in a number of ways including the hiding of in-demand and reference material, theft or mutilation of documents and disruptive or abusive behaviour as a result of frustration, impatience and alienation. Whilst not condoning such activities, a lack of support at the time of need is one element which can lead a small minority to behave antisocially.

In order to address the problem of library services to individual staff and students, a number of strategies may be adopted. Two particular strategies – the readers' enquiry service and current awareness/alerting services – are developed in some detail later.

Appointments or surgeries
In some libraries a system of booking appointments with subject/faculty librarians or holding regular surgeries have succeeded in addressing individual information problems – or, indeed, those of small groups – effectively but not efficiently. Unless the library is generously and suitably staffed, this service can only cope with the tip of the iceberg.

Convergence
Well over half of UK University libraries now form part of a converged service. Convergence between libraries, computing services and other central support agencies continues apace although there is a variety of models to choose from. One of the potential advantages of operational convergence is the more comprehensive assistance which can be offered to individuals. Increasingly, there are examples where enquiry points are staffed by those with multiple skills – hybrids who have built up skills in computing and related areas as well as information retrieval and management. This notion of providing a 'seamless' service at a one stop shop – this mix of technical advice and informational guidance – is one that individuals seeking support undoubtedly find attractive. Most users are not interested in the organisational structure or who actually offers the help, as long as the help provided is effective.

Customer focus
This emphasis on the importance of the customer or user has become part of the culture of many public service organisations, including many academic libraries. Implicit in a library's approach to customer orientation is the paramount importance of aiming to satisfy the information needs of the individual. Customer care training and statements (see Appendix VI) are helping to reinforce this attitude both for the users and the library staff. As issue and enquiry services take on a more frantic air, living up to a customer care statement is certainly a challenge!

Readers' enquiry and current awareness/alerting services are two very different examples of services tailored for individuals. The first is aimed primarily at students, the second at academic staff and researchers.

Readers' enquiry services

To offer an efficient and effective reference and enquiry service is to focus on the specific needs of one individual – from simple directional help to complex subject-based information retrieval. In these days of mass further and higher education it is recognised as a genuinely user-centred approach to service provision. The nature of enquiry work places many demands on library staff but particularly on their time. This staff-intensive work is often viewed by academic and library staff as the main interface between user and library other than the issue and return of books. Ironically, this service – potentially expensive in terms of the staffing budget – tends to be overshadowed in the professional literature in favour of other more fashionable topics such as information skills training and almost anything IT-related. It is important to ensure a high quality enquiry service for both economic and educational reasons. The paucity of professional comment may be explained partly by the nature of the interpersonal skills required by the librarian and possibly by the complexity of the enquiry interview. It is interesting to note that there is much more written about reference and enquiry services in North American literature than there is in the UK. As is shown later in this chapter the literature on the evaluation of enquiry services is more forthcoming.

A reference and enquiry service is an integral part of most academic library services. Conceptually, it sits comfortably amongst circulation, collection provision, user education, IT facilities and support literature. Its relationship with user education has been the subject of some debate over the last twenty years. Some have argued [2] that reference and enquiry work is what librarians do best and that user education requires skills that are alien to many librarians. This is too simplistic and defeatist. They are complementary activities each of which demands different skills. [3] Students, for example, who have experienced enlightening and stimulating user education programmes often come away enthused and motivated. They then ask questions at enquiry points or of subject/faculty librarians prompted directly or indirectly by the programmes. Similarly, questions may be raised in the minds of students when they have had time to reflect on the content of such programmes. The volume and nature of enquiries will depend largely on the success of other library service elements. The provision of a collection of material which falls short of meeting academic community needs is likely to generate more enquiries. Helpful support literature in the form of general and specific guides, 'crib-sheets' and workbooks together with effective signposting will aim to increase user independence. Some current computer catalogues are guilty of posing more questions than they answer: arcane cataloguing principles, inadequate help screens and a plethora of fines and loan regimes. Why are we surprised at user confusion? Perhaps even more worrying is the number of users who choose, for whatever reasons, not to seek clarification on these things at enquiry points or elsewhere.

It makes sense to put these services under the coordinating eye of a senior member of the library staff, particularly in a large library. The elements for coordination could include the following:

Policy and guidelines

- There should be a requirement for an enquiry service policy and guidelines. This will help in the operation of a consistent and equitable service. It will help with matters such as referrals, the 'show versus do' approach, and the conduct expected of staff.

Staff training

- All those staffing enquiry points need to attain a certain level of competence and master a variety of skills in both general and subject-based enquiries.

Staff rostering

- Issues here include sharing workloads, covering staff in times of absence, multiple service points, avoiding long stretches at enquiry desks at stressful periods, coverage during all available opening hours and providing a balanced staffing mix of functional and subject expertise.

Monitor and review

- This may include record keeping, collecting and submitting statistics, checking on targets or standards, carrying out surveys or observing for staff appraisal.

The enquiry interview

What?

The terminology surrounding enquiry work is varied. Readers' enquiries, (customer) information desk, enquiry point, reference and information service, information desk, 'knocking on the librarian's door' and many more are all in current use. At the most basic level these refer to the enquiry – usually face-to-face but also through other channels – in which the user is given personal assistance in the pursuit of information. In the typical academic library the range of enquiry categories is diverse. They include the following:

- Directional
  e.g. 'Where are the microbiology journals?'

- Policy/procedural
  e.g. 'Can I renew these books over the telephone?'

- Catalogue-related
  e.g. 'Can I search for a book on the catalogue without knowing the author's name?'

- Factual
  e.g. 'What is the population of Luxembourg?'

- Subject-specific
  e.g. 'I need to find out what has been written in the last five years about teleconferencing'.

- Technical/equipment-related
  e.g. 'Could you help me download this article on to my floppy disc?'

Naturally, there could be considerable overlap between categories and a variety of combinations in any one enquiry interview. But the key point is the expectation on the part of the enquirer that the librarian will satisfy the whole range. The more protracted enquiry may be postponed or referred to another colleague or agency, although a start may be made on it at the enquiry point.

Where?

Enquiries can take place in a variety of locations or through different communication channels:

- via telephone, letter, fax or e-mail

- at the issue or circulation desk (which may double as an enquiry point in a smaller campus library)

- at a designated information service point

- at the subject enquiry point (which may be separate from the above and staffed by librarians with particular subject-related expertise)

- in the librarian's office or at his or her desk (where these enquiries may be encouraged; indeed in some libraries, as in other professions, regular surgeries are held).

The service may be provided in a number of these ways and may involve more than one librarian or other agency. At some service points, particularly during busy periods, the presence of more than one librarian is essential. It is important to ensure that, wherever possible, any enquiry point:

- is identifiable

- is accessible

- commands a good view of library activity

- is situated near to computer catalogues, equipment, reference collecions
- is staffed appropriately
- is suitably equipped and furnished.

Who?

This type of work requires qualified and preferably experienced librarians. Of course, experience comes with time and therefore the library needs to have an established staff development and training programme for all those involved in these activities. This aspect is explored later.

In recent years the changing nature of further and higher education has demanded a more intensive enquiry service with changing emphases. Firstly, students are encouraged to become more self-reliant in their learning habits and many have become less dependent on tutors. This educational change – inevitably sends greater numbers of students to the library. Even with a higher profile given to user education programmes students may feel intimidated by the size and complexity of service provision. Readers' enquiry points and one-to-one tutorials thus form an essential point-of-need service. Secondly, the increasing pace of technological change has further complicated the information-seeking process. The newer technologies such as metropolitan and global networking are combining with anachronistic and at times troublesome microform equipment whilst pressure on photocopying facilities continues unabated. PC-based and multimedia packages alongside specialist open access databases complete a daunting scene for the uninitiated. On top of this, hopes and expectations are being raised for the Internet and World Wide Web as sources of information for academic libraries.

It is against this background that the librarian's personal qualities need to be assessed. They will be as important to an effective service as qualifications and experience. The qualities sought include:

- willingness to help
- approachability
- confidence
- enthusiasm
- positive attitude
- adaptability
- tolerance
- patience
- courtesy
- sensitivity

- resourcefulness
- persistence
- imagination
- intuition
- caring disposition
- impartiality
- a sense of humour!

The likelihood of discovering all these qualities in one body is, perhaps, remote. However, the recruiter of staff who will work at an enquiry point needs to consider such individual qualities very carefully.

The complexity of current enquiry service provision has enabled a number of libraries to adopt a two-part system. This involves the provision of an initial service point to act as an information 'filter' or gateway. The librarian at this point would perhaps require skills different from those working at the subject enquiry points. Many of the simple directional requests can be filtered out at this stage and the more complex subject enquiries referred as appropriate to other service points or colleagues. Some libraries employ an enquiry point that is devoted to technical, equipment or IT-related problems. This is often the case in those universities that have converged library and computing services. This type of arrangement has been taken a stage further in the USA with a variety of enquiry point levels. [4]

Practicalities of enquiry service provision

In order to negotiate successfully – for both parties – the four stages of the enquiry interview outlined below, a certain amount of preparation and groundwork is necessary. There can, of course, be no guarantee of success in an activity so heavily dependent on the skills, knowledge and attitudes of the individuals involved.

Stages

1. The library user perceives a library or information related problem.

2. If the user decides to approach an enquiry point, he or she needs to formulate the problem into words to explain it clearly to library staff.

3. If appropriate, discussion takes place to clarify the requirements of the user.

4. The user is either provided with the solution or a means to a solution.

Many of the following points could be usefully made available to all relevant staff in the form of an enquiry procedures and policy manual. The following sections cover the possible contents of such a manual.

Enquiries policy

It is advisable that the library have a policy on the type of service it wishes to provide to the academic community. This may include the 'show versus do' philosophy, that is whether you show the enquirer how to find the information or you yourself get the information for the enquirer. This would only apply in the case of more complex enquiries. Most academic libraries would lean naturally to the educationally sound 'show' approach whereby library staff would assist users to find the required information through guidance. Such an approach may also involve instruction in particular search methods or in navigating around databases. The rationale is similar to that underpinning the transferable skills programme in Chapter 3. If the user understands the process of solving the problem, he or she will be able to transfer the same principles to another parallel situation. A cynic may also suggest that this approach may mean one less enquiry for the future! Inevitably, there are occasions when straightforward factfinding is necessary and the librarian takes the shortest route to the solution. The enquirer may or may not be concerned about the source. The increased pressure placed on enquiry services at peak times during the day or year is forcing a more pragmatic approach from both sides. Often the user needs the information urgently and it is the product rather than the process that is important. Similarly, the librarian faced with a queue of irritated users can realistically spend only limited time with each. This type of situation provides a challenge to the librarian aiming to instruct! In reality the outcomes will be reached through a combination of factfinding, help and instruction with the boundaries very often blurred.

Priorities

The library staff need to be clear about service priorities. Examples could include the following:

- give priority to the enquirer in front of you. If the telephone rings and no other librarian is available, it should either be allowed to ring or an answering machine should be used

- if a queue builds up, concentrate your attention on the enquiry and avoid being diverted by expressions of frustration or irritation. Naturally, help should be sought when necessary or convenient and if available

- give priority to serving the users rather than your own administrative tasks. How many times do users approach an enquiry point with the words 'I'm sorry to disturb you. Could you tell me . . .'

- do not wait to be approached if you see a student who is obviously in need of assistance

- put yourself in the place of the enquirer and imagine your own feelings.

Staff training

The skills, knowledge and attitudes required for the successful resolution of enquiries are many. However, certain staff development and training courses – both in-house and externally arranged – can go a long way to help staff achieve levels of competence and develop appropriate attitudes for enquiry work. These include:

- courses run by recognised bodies such as the Library Association, Aslib and TFPL on handling reference enquiries. These are usually tailored to suit both newcomers to the profession and more experienced staff. Topics include interpersonal skills (customer care, telephone manner etc.), dealing with a variety of enquiries and administration

- in-house training programmes for the induction of new library staff or updating the knowledge and skills of existing staff. Such programmes would include:

  – database workshop

  – reference material seminars

  – new equipment, hardware/software packages

  – new services e.g. services to non-traditional students or self-renewal

  – new automated functions eg acquisitions or interlibrary loans

  – regular refresher courses.

All the above could be carried out by the appropriate subject or functional librarians, technicians or other members of staff. Training programmes can take place either before the library opens, during a closed period specifically for this purpose or repeated later in the week so as to cover everyone in two sessions. Refresher courses could be run every term or semester depending on the amount of change taking place. Where librarians staff enquiry desks out in the library (as opposed to subject surgeries in their offices), there needs to be an agreed, consistent level of service. The requirement that appropriate librarians keep themselves updated on sources relating to subject areas outside their own would be paramount but difficult to achieve.

- Librarians new to the service would benefit from shadowing an experienced reference and enquiry librarian or from observing interaction at the enquiry points. The use of a standard checklist with space for comments may be appropriate. The checklist could include type of enquiry, time taken and sources used. Later discussions with mentor or line manager may also prove beneficial

- It may be helpful for staff to keep a personal log of their enquiry work to include useful new sources, solutions, tips, short cuts, advice. These can be updated and reviewed periodically

- Where staff appraisal operates, observation of enquiry work may be appropriate particularly with a view to staff development.

Technical support

The rapid developments in information technology are being reflected increasingly in a change of emphasis at the library/enquirer interface. Nowadays the pervasive nature of these services allows only a minority of users to avoid coming into contact with them. Although cohorts going through post-sixteen education are becoming more computer-literate, there remain many users who feel apprehensive about libraries generally and about IT more specifically. Enquiry services are available to assist in such situations. Technicians may also be available for troubleshooting purposes. The topical university policy of offering converged services to users highlights the importance of clear lines of communication. [5]Examples of potential tensions include:

- when to report technical faults, since certain basic procedures can be attempted first

- to whom to report technical faults and what to do when they are unavailable

- the likely timescale for rectifying the fault

- what to do when the fault is likely to be long term

- the use of appropriate signs for faulty equipment or facilities

- the procedure for informing other relevant parties about a fault – in terms of immediate need to know and also for the purpose of monitoring IT equipment failure

- feeding back information to users in a sensitive way.

Referrals

Referring users to other librarians, academic staff or other agencies forms a necessary but at times neglected stage in meeting information needs. The enquiry point does, after all, act as a gateway and cannot answer all questions at the time of need. Although some users may have unrealistic expectations about the kind of enquiry service provided by the library, an efficient and effective referral system is generally acceptable. However, the following points need to be borne in mind:

- all avenues should be explored before referral

- the librarian should not be seen to 'pass the buck'

- if a referral is made to a colleague within the building or on a nearby campus, this person should be contacted to check availability, clarify the nature of the request and arrange an appointment if necessary

- a pro-forma sheet (see Appendix VII) containing all relevant details should be completed before referral.

Support literature

Enquiry staff should endeavour to have access to a comprehensive range of high quality support literature. This type of publication can often solve an information problem very quickly. There is a wide variety of point-of-need publications. Here are examples of the main types, some of which have been described in more detail in Chapter 2:

- general guides to the library

- subject-specific guides

- guides to special collections

- guides to special services

- guides for non-traditional students

- guides to Internet resources

- lists of databases

- lists of audiovisual material

- lists of journals

- lists of new acquisitions

- lists of abstracting/indexing services

- how to use the library catalogues

- library bulletins

- instructional sheets for online services

- workbooks

- journal contents pages

- bibliographies

- bookmarks

It is helpful not only to display these publications prominently but also to make them available as a central databank (for library staff) so that enquiry points may be continually 'topped up'. A copy of each may also be distributed more widely to appropriate staff.

Administration

For enquiry points to function successfully, the administrative wheels have to be oiled frequently. The following are suggestions which will help to smooth daily operations:

- designate a member of staff or a group of staff to ensure daily administration of and responsibility for enquiry points. Alternatively, the task could form part of a rostering system
- operate a daily log book to register faults, action points, hot topics, so that subsequent staff are fully informed
- operate a list/index of frequently asked questions (FAQs)
- ensure a continuous supply of stationery, support literature, spare discs, print cartridges etc
- where appropriate, ensure stationery and equipment for users, for example staplers, guillotines, scissors, tape etc
- provide a set of name badges for individual members of staff or name cards for desks.

Evaluation of enquiry services

To provide a realistic picture of the efficiency and effectiveness of an enquiry service, there are two levels of evaluation:

- character and volume of enquiries
- quality, accuracy and competence of the service.

Quantitative evaluation

The first level consists of mainly quantitative data for the purposes of management decision-making or for external agencies such as SCONUL. The concern with collecting such statistics is the clarification of what constitutes an enquiry, for example, are directional enquiries included?

A count may be made in terms of the following:

- enquiries during a given time period
- duration of enquiries

- enquiries at particular service points

- category of question; e.g. factual, catalogue-related etc.

- category of user, such as department, course, mode of attendance

- sources used to satisfy enquiry.

Care needs to be taken to include *all* enquiry transactions – at various service points, in offices etc. Other counting periods may include quiet and busy times, separate floors or rooms, specific days or vacation periods.

Qualitative evaluation

The above statistics do not, however, provide a qualitative evaluation of the service's effectiveness. Surveys and tests are the two main methods for this purpose.

Tests
Since the mid-1960s unobtrusive testing has been carried out mainly in the United States to gauge the accuracy of responses.[6,7] For the purposes of academic libraries this method has been largely discredited. The reasons are concerned with measurement of only one small part of the enquiry service (such as factual answers); the sometimes secondary nature of interpersonal skills; users being partially satisfied with responses; and, finally, the ethics of such an exercise, which may make library staff feel uneasy or suspicious. Recently, however this 'mystery shopping' approach has been revived successfully by Town.[8] Town undertook a large-scale benchmarking exercise which made successful use of unobtrusive testing in the form of reference questions put to staff at enquiry points.

Satisfaction surveys
Although they have their own inherent problems, including user expectations and attitude measurement, satisfaction surveys undoubtedly yield the most useful data on service effectiveness. This example covers evaluation of the results of the enquiry and also the conduct and attitude of the librarian. It thus aims to cover the process of the encounter rather than focusing only on the outcome.

For optimum response rates questionnaires should be short and unambiguous. They should be distributed at all appropriate service points by people trained in the art of polite, friendly persuasion. A decision needs to be made about:

- the hoped-for number of responses. From this the approximate number for distribution is known based on a 60% response rate for previous readers' enquiry surveys.

- the period during which the survey is to take place.

- whether a sampling procedure is appropriate.

Current awareness and alerting services

There is a variety of mechanisms by which academic staff can be alerted to information which is relevant to their professional interests or which helps to provide an improved service to the users (through help with materials selection etc.). Rather than offering a traditional current awareness service – and this may be appropriate for some libraries – as described by Hamilton[9] and Whitehall,[10] in our view alerting services constitute a wider type of service which encompasses any of the following elements:

- newsletters or bulletins

- lists of new acquisitions

- journal contents pages

- current awareness or SDI services

- electronic alerting services

- circulation of journals

- publisher and other trade catalogues

- network resources.

The range of services naturally depends on a multitude of variables such as the size and ethos of institution and library; the library's profile within institution, the library's staffing structure; the perceived importance of such services; the degree of integration and level of liaison activity between library and departments. In addition, the move towards more user-centred teaching and learning methods, together with technological developments, has enabled a number of electronic alerting services to be introduced. In some libraries these services have been perceived as a source of tension. On the one hand part of the librarian's role is to offer an alerting service to academic staff. On the other hand there are increasing opportunities for individuals to update and alert *themselves*. These services such as Blackwell's UnCover, the British Library's Inside Information and the BIDS contents page provision represent the continuing move by commercial organisations to target the end users, to aim services and facilities directly at the academic community. Their availability and accessibility will vary according to library and institutional policies. Some may be available within the library or networked across sites, others may be accessible within academic departments, computer rooms or academic staff offices. In other organisations it may have been decided not to subscribe to any of these types of service. Is there a danger of the librarian becoming peripheral to requirements? We believe not, as the librarian's role in relation to these services is one of sponsor, providing advice and guidance to individuals. Academic librarians can still learn from staff and researchers about their methods of searching and retrieving information, as well as about the application of these services to teaching and research. It should be viewed as an opportunity not a threat.

So what are the advantages of providing alerting services?

- Particularly for the academic librarian who is new to the post, these services offer an ideal opportunity to foster a healthy relationship with a specific group of users. As an example, the first thing one of the authors did on arriving in a Subject Librarian's post at a college was to establish a new acquisitions and journal contents pages service. Since this exercise entailed the rapid accumulation of user profiles it succeeded in both orientating the new appointee to the academic staff and their research and teaching interests and providing a valuable service (as subsequent evaluation confirmed).

- Such services provide regular relevant updating for hard-pressed individuals who may have limited time to keep abreast of local or wider developments. Alerting services offer a structured formal way of achieving this if carried out efficiently and effectively. It is important for the librarians to gain the confidence of the individuals or groups in providing a value-added service. A thorough knowledge of subject-based sources and technological developments is an essential prerequisite to gaining credibility within the academic community (see Chapter 7).

- It is important to offer a valued *specific* service to individuals so that the idea of 'service' becomes built into the institutional and library ethos. In recent years there has been much debate about the importance of customers and their needs. This is one example of tailoring a service tightly to the needs of an individual or group. The outcome is that the individual recipients benefit from the focused service and the library enhances its reputation for being proactive. It assimilates libraries more deeply into research and teaching projects within academic departments. This latter move represents another level at which the integration discussed in Chapter 3 may be assisted.

- A user interest profile whereby staff and researchers register their subject interests, membership of associations, and journal subscriptions can provide in a comprehensive and formal way a working tool to help with material selection, forwarding or networking of useful sources. Naturally, any such profile needs to be updated regularly with new subject areas and new lecturers and new researchers.

- Alerting services, particularly those available through CD-ROMs or via online hosts, can often act as a focus and a catalyst for sharing expertise, experience and ideas. The librarian's role becomes that of a gatekeeper.

Workshops organised by the library staff for academic departments may provide the initial impetus for usage of the services.

- The more widespread use of electronic mail, uploading and downloading of files has facilitated more straightforward dissemination of relevant information. A number of libraries make use of bibliographic software such as Pro-Cite to save time and improve the final product. The end user is becoming increasingly accustomed to communicating at the desktop or place of need. The facility for incorporating more alerting services in the networking infrastructure will inevitably increase in the coming years. The development of SuperJANET, Metropolitan Area Networks (MANs) on top of Local Area Networks (LANs) should ensure improved speed and volume of access and also quality of graphics and interfaces.

User interest profiles

Before embarking on any kind of alerting service, it is essential to become acquainted with the research and teaching interests of the groups or individual users. This exercise may be carried out through informal discussions. However, it is advisable to formalise the process through the circulation of a standard profile sheet. Appendix VIII shows an example. It is worth spending some time compiling an accurate comprehensive profile so that alerting services will be focused effectively. To take into account developing and modifying research programmes as well as staff teaching on different courses, profiles need to be updated at least annually. Some textbooks advise that interviews should follow the receipt of profile sheets. This may be a necessary step in some cases; however, time constraints would inhibit any wider discussions.

Practicalities of providing alerting services

Having decided that these services may provide benefits to members of your institution, it is worth considering a selection in more detail.

Newsletter/Bulletin

The newsletter is a suitable method for some communication purposes and, if the use of e-mail is widespread, this may be the preferred medium. The content of a regular newsletter or bulletin will depend on the needs of the academic staff and researchers. Examples may include the promotion of new library services, new developments and databases, new journals (new either to the world or to the library), conferences, local initiatives and projects. Newsletters which are sharp and concise would be particularly suited to e-mail format. These may then be read, archived, copied, forwarded, printed or deleted. With most e-mail systems the process of establishing circulation groups is fairly straightforward. An up-to-date user profile will help with this. Newsletters can also be distributed to the libraries of associated institutions, for example where franchise or access courses are taught. Communicating in this way can often help to allay feelings of isolation or marginalisation which may arise in these cooperative arrangements. A combination of newsletter and another type of publication (such as a new acquisitions list) may also be desirable.

New acquisitions
Lists of newly acquired material may be provided separately or combined as suggested above. Most of the integrated computer systems available in contemporary academic libraries have the capacity to generate a whole range of management information including, for example, lists of new books. Such lists can usually be sorted and printed in a variety of formats using appropriate wordprocessing packages. They may then be either printed and distributed to those on a circulation list, e-mailed to groups of staff or uploaded on to a central electronic facility such as a specific networked disc-drive or a campus wide information service (CWIS). For those libraries that rely on manually generated lists, there are benefits to be gained from an extensive time commitment. Such a service can also generate debate about material selection policies and budgetary matters.

Journal contents pages
One way in which academic staff keep abreast of developments and activities within their subject areas is to scan the contents pages of the appropriate journal literature. Electronic tables of contents have already been referred to and are covered below. Although an established service in many libraries, the popularity and usefulness of photocopied contents' pages should not be underestimated. Such a service may also raise issues concerning journal subscriptions (including gaps in provision and underuse), database provision and journal indexing services. Appendix IX shows an example of a questionnaire distributed to academic staff to evaluate a combined acquisitions/contents page bulletin.

Current awareness/SDI service
Traditionally, a current awareness service is provided for a specific user group. Rowley's[11] definition is a sound one:

> 'A current awareness service is intended to keep professionals up-to-date in areas that are of interest to them and which may impinge upon their professional activities'

An SDI service represents a more personal service and is extensively provided in commercial and specialised library and information services. Individuals receive regular notifications of new literature and developments in accordance with interest profiles. In the past these have been carried out through the manual in-house scanning of relevant sources or via online hosts. Some organisations provide group

SDI services which are broadly similar to current awareness services. While the use of online hosts for these purposes has decreased due to the widespread use of CD-ROM and other networking services, a helpful account of these facilities on hosts such as Dialog and Datastar is given by Rowley.[11] The criteria for evaluating such services would include subject coverage, currency, costs, format of output, document delivery and relevance.

In-house scanning of sources within further and higher education is becoming less viable as staff time becomes more expensive, less available, and electronic services proliferate. It is difficult to justify such services other than on a limited scale or for a specific project.

Electronic alerting services
These services, known as Current Alerting Services-Individual Article Supply (CAS-IAS), have begun to proliferate during this decade. A number of database producers combine the current awareness facility with the rapid delivery of the required document. Longer established ones include Inside Information, launched by the British Library in 1993, UnCover, originally a collaborative venture between Blackwells and CARL and launched in 1991, and Swetscan which began in 1993. Tables of contents are also searchable on the Institute of Scientific Information (ISI) databases mounted on BIDS and therefore potentially available to academic staff and students. In the latter example users are able to save searches and rerun them at a later date. Documents are supplied at a price within twenty four hours if required. Woodward [12] provides an evaluative account of the major CAS-IAS services. Aston University Library is currently undertaking a British Library funded research project to investigate the functionality, costs, value and impact of these services.

Circulation of journals
Circulation of journals can be effective in smaller college libraries and amongst small closed groups of users such as researchers. A list of interested parties is attached to the front cover of the journal and a 'pass the parcel' method is used. The problem of the journal's unavailability in the library may be obviated by displaying it for a specific period of time before circulation, perhaps one week. If the material is circulated around less than six people, its currency is retained. This method may also be appropriate for the circulation of sample copies of new journals. Either promotional copies of new journals are sent to appropriate library staff or librarians may make a point of obtaining samples of new journal titles gleaned from the media, publishers' catalogues and the professional press. Either way the academic staff or researchers can be alerted to these publications according to their subject interests.

Publisher and trade catalogues
Librarians are inevitably placed on a variety of external mailing lists and particularly on those of publishers. Many of these catalogues can be circulated to interested parties for the purposes of inclusion in research and teaching programmes, borrowing from other libraries or purchasing. Similarly, groups of users may be alerted to new material through bibliographies or relevant sections thereof, for example *British National Bibliography (BNB),* through lists of new journal titles, such as those provided by Blackwells, and through lists of new books organised by class numbers, for example Dawson's lists. These are examples of opportunities for the tightly controlled circulation of information potentially useful to particular groups and, via the library, to other groups with wider interests.

Network Resources
The increase in the gateway and filtering role of the academic librarian is at its most influential when applied to the Internet. The 'network of networks' has enabled particular groups of researchers, academic staff and librarians to become part of a larger and more focused 'virtual community'. This represents one way in which mutual alerting services can develop. Where the subject interests of each of the constituents are known, relevant sources may be forwarded and downloaded to disc. Until navigation around the Internet becomes a more structured operation – and recent improvements in search engines indicate that progress is being made – this sharing of source information can be an effective method of establishing expertise, knowledge and confidence. The facility on some software packages such as Netscape to 'bookmark' or archive sources that are relevant provides an easy-to-use method of sharing addresses or universal resource locators (URLs).

Conclusion

The inclusion of these two types of service – enquiry services and alerting services – is aimed at emphasising the importance of supporting library users as individuals. Increasingly, these individuals are not required to present themselves physically at the library. Support is often provided at the end of a telephone, fax, e-mail or through direct dial-up services. It is important to remember that students are individuals, not full-time equivalents, and they have a variety of needs, including information needs, over the duration of their courses. Alerting services represent an attempt by librarians to support individual academic staff and researchers. In so doing they can relieve some of the growing pressure and shortage of time experienced by most staff working in higher education.

References

1. Reichel, M. Twenty-five year retrospection: the importance of what we do. *RQ,* 33(3), 1993, pp.30–35.

2. Lester, R. Why educate the user? *Aslib Proceedings,* 31(8), 1979, pp366 – 380.

3. Rettig, J. The convergence of the twain or titanic collision? Bibliographic instruction and reference in the 1990s sea of change. *Reference Services Review,* 23(1), 1995, pp.7–20.

4. Whitson, W.L. Differentiated service: a new reference model. *Journal of Academic Librarianship,* , 21(2), 1995, pp.103 – 111.

5. Williams, A.G. Where are we going? The development of convergence between university libraries and computing services *In* Harris, C. *ed. The new university library: issues for the 90s and beyond.* London: Taylor Graham, 1994, pp.55–72.

6. Williams, R. An unobtrusive survey of academic library reference services. Library and *Information Research News,* 1987, 10 (37/38) pp12 – 40.

7. McClure, C.R. and Hernon, P. *Improving the quality of reference service for government publications.* Chicago: American Library Association, 1983.

8. Town, S. *Benchmarking in libraries: a report on the Royal Military College Shrivenham Project.* Cranfield University: RMCS Information Services, 1995.

9. Hamilton, F. *Current awareness, current techniques.* Aldershot: Gower, 1995.

10. Whitehall, T., ed. *Practical current awareness services for libraries.* Aldershot: Gower, 1986.

11. Rowley, J. Current awareness and the online hosts in Raitt, D.I. *ed. Online Information 92: 16th International Online Information Meeting Proceedings, London 8 – 10 December 1992.* Oxford: Learned Information, 1993, pp.251–262.

12. Woodward, H. The impact of electronic information on serials collection management. *Serials,* 7(1), 1994, pp.29–36.

5. Library services to non-traditional students

'Unless you conduct yourselves with more restraint and moderation towards them [overseas students]*, they will be driven into abandoning their studies and leaving the country...'*
Henry III to the citizens of Cambridge in 1231

Across further and higher education there is a growing interest in how institutions can more effectively support the growing numbers of non-traditional students. It is the purpose of this chapter to suggest ways in which academic libraries can play their part in enhancing levels of service to these students.

First of all it is worth reflecting on the term 'non-traditional students'. It is an awkward term, largely because it is not good practice to define any group of people by a negative. It immediately implies a lower status than those 'traditional' students who presumably form the core of UK further and higher education. Yet such an inference would be quite incorrect.

Traditional students can be defined as follows:

- young, typically aged between 18 and 22
- studying full-time
- living away from home
- having reasonably good A-levels grades
- taking a degree in one or two subject disciplines
- having good study skills
- having adequate with good contact with the academic staff
- following a traditional pattern of higher education that is built around lectures and tutorials.

It is fair to state that the deployment and roles of academic staff and the organisation of higher education institutions are based upon this established model. Careers services, refectories, libraries, chaplaincies, administration and academic life are largely designed to support this traditional form of higher education. There is a deep-seated belief that this form of higher education is right and proper; that it is indeed the core of UK higher education.

However, the traditional pattern of higher education is subject to very considerable change. Young, full-time students are themselves experiencing changes in the kind of education they undertake. The considerable growth in student numbers has changed the nature of the full-time student body, who may, for example, be from wider social backgrounds and have less confidence in their academic abilities or their financial security. The expansion of modular programmes has changed the settled pattern of degree work. For example, the number of students taking multidisciplinary studies has increased considerably. There is much less contact between tutors and full-time students. The rise of skills-based education, particularly in professional subjects such as Law, has rendered success at A-level less of a guarantee of success at degree level. Despite widespread and perhaps nostalgic attachment to a traditional model of higher education, the reality is one of change.

Another major change in higher education is the growth in the numbers of non-traditional students. These may be defined as those students who are:

- mature, i.e. over 25 years of age
- studying part-time
- distance learners
- on franchised courses in FE colleges
- from overseas
- disabled or with special needs
- entering education via new routes, such as Access courses.

In fact, in UK higher education DFE statistics show that these 'non-traditional' students now form the majority:

- in 1992 a student population of 2,333,000 comprised 841,300 full-time students, 567,700 part-time students, 924,000 students on Continuing Education or other HE level short courses
- mature students entering higher education doubled between 1982 and 1992 to 319,000, which is 53% of the total
- in addition, in 1992 there were 90,000 overseas students and an estimated 40,000 students with disabilities.

Furthermore, the academic achievements of mature, part-time students are impressive. The 26-30 year old age group perform better academically than any other; and the highest proportion of first-class honours is in the 30-34 age group. This is despite the fact that a majority of part-time students have entry qualifications other than A-levels.

It has been argued by Tight that the pattern of UK higher education since 1945, far from being traditional, is in fact an aberration.[1] In other words, the recent growth in non-traditional students represents a return to earlier forms of education, such as correspondence courses, professional studies and external degrees. It can also be argued that recent changes are bringing UK higher education into line with that of other countries. One further reason for change is that universities are increasingly pursuing local, regional and industrial strategies, and these must inevitably lead to a further increase in non-traditional students. Furthermore it is now widely recognised that education must become something that continues throughout life. The goal of lifelong learning can only be achieved through non-traditional forms of study.

The characteristics of non-traditional students

The first characteristic of non-traditional students is their sheer diversity. This can be seen in the various groups that together comprise 'non-traditional' students. For example, franchise students are very different from overseas students. However, even within one group of students there can be considerable differences between individual students. For example, part-time students who attend classes one or two evenings a week are very different from distance-learners who rarely, if ever, visit their universities. Vocationally-oriented part-time students are typically males in the late 20s or early 30s studying technical or business subjects. They can be differentiated from personally-oriented part-time students, who are typically female, in their 30s or 40s and studying arts or social science subjects. Some mature students will have excellent academic track records and be studying for the simple enjoyment of doing so. They may well be quite self-sufficient. 'Second chance' students, however, are experiencing higher education for the first time and may have rather rusty study skills.

Other students may experience cultural difficulties. Most obviously, this will apply to the large number of overseas students present in Britain each year. It is now understood that the problems that face these students are not due to their reluctance to adapt to our traditional systems. They are due to the inability of educational institutions to provide appropriate support that meets the needs of a significant group of students. Such cultural problems are of course not unique to students from other countries. UK students from a wide range of backgrounds may find the way of life of a university difficult to cope with.

There are a number of characteristics that are shared by a large number of non-traditional students. One of these is the shortage of time that affects so many part-time, mature and distance learning students. Shortage of time often arises from other commitments, particularly those of job and childcare. Responsibilities and commitments can cause difficulties around transport to and from college or university. Time management can become a real issue, for example simply in finding time to study, to use libraries or to discuss study matters with fellow students. The pressures arising out of lack of time can lead to genuine anxieties.

Many of the problems of time management that face non-traditional students are overcome because students often show an unusual degree of motivation and commitment. Mature students are often self-directed, resourceful, responsive and keen to do well. However, despite enthusiasm and hard work, non-traditional students can also have inadequate study skills. They can find libraries 'daunting' or they may find essay writing difficult. This can be a particular problem for distance learners, who are required to have the ability to learn effectively with little support from others. [2]

For a number of reasons, therefore, non-traditional students may need support and encouragement. They also need to be able to communicate effectively with lecturing and support staff. They need to be able to explain their circumstances, and to meet with a sympathetic response that is prepared, when necessary, to bend rules and regulations. They may best be supported by means of a flexible response from university or college staff.

Finally, another characteristic of many non-traditional students is a desire to get value for money. This may be ascribed to a general rise of 'charterism' in society, or to the greater awareness of civil rights that characterises people with disabilities. Older students are often very conscious that they – or their employers – are paying considerable fees for an educational qualification that requires tremendous commitment on their part. They will, therefore, be rightly intolerant of poor quality teaching or poor services. One can only agree with them, that where serious difficulties do occur they are not 'problems of part-time students' or 'the problem overseas students'. They are the result of problems in higher education institutions that are slow to adapt to the growing numbers of non-traditional students. The remainder of this chapter will show ways in which academic libraries can improve their services so as to provide non-traditional students with the levels of service to which they are entitled.

Services to users with disabilities

There are no exact figures for the numbers of disabled students in UK higher education, though there are estimated to be some 40,000. However, what is indisputable is that this particular group of non-traditional students is certain to grow. People with disabilities are now emerging from mainstream secondary education, and they have much higher expectations than many of their forebears who were educated separately. They are motivated by a desire for the benefits of education, and by a real concern for their civil rights. The growing assertiveness of disabled people concerning their rights to equality of opportunity is being seen throughout society.

What does the term 'disability' mean in practice? In fact the symbol for disability – the wheelchair – is rather misleading. Only 7% of people with disabilities use a wheelchair. Although it is common for people in higher education to consider problems of physical access, this is not the primary concern of disabled students. Above all, these students need high quality services from colleges and universities. Inadequate physical access is, therefore, not a reason for institutions or their libraries not providing services to students with special needs.

There is much that librarians can do to help disabled users, even where their libraries were not designed with the needs of such users in mind.

Designate a specialist member or members of staff

It is essential that disabled users have a specified contact person who is able to spend time helping them get what they need from the library. Library specialists can be of two kinds. Firstly, they may be employed at an operational level. For example, a library assistant can have responsibility for helping users with a Kurzweil voice synthesiser, or for getting books from shelves for people in wheelchairs. Secondly, it is useful to have someone with managerial responsibilities for the service to disabled staff and students. Such a person will push for the development of the service, for example by seeking resources for new equipment or by pressing for the library's staff development programme to include deaf awareness training. These specialist staff members may or may not have other duties and responsibilities, probably depending upon the size and resource levels of the library. What is essential is that they are present in the library for students to go to seek help or advice. In the case of disabled students this is particularly important as they will sometimes wish to discuss confidential or personal matters with a member of library staff whom they can trust.

Provide training and awareness for library staff

The good work of specialist staff needs to be supported by the rest of the library staff. This requires that staff understand the needs of people with certain disabilities. The importance of this question has been shown by recent American research which revealed that only 50% of academic librarians had a positive disposition towards users with disabilities.[3]

It is interesting to note that females and younger librarians (under 30) had the best attitudes. Training for library staff will teach them to face deaf students who lip read and to use special registration procedures for students who cannot read or fill in forms. Library staff need to be able to recognise the difficulties that some dyslexic students have with the dewey Decimal system and other classification schemes (or indeed with signs and number sequences generally).

Understand the needs of students

The needs of disabled students will vary greatly, so understanding their needs may not be straightforward. It may well be time consuming. However, it is an essential prerequisite to providing a good service. The US librarian D.E. Jones has stated that disabled students have three categories of needs:

1.Comfort and safety needs
This could include braille labels on coffee vending machines or fire alarms for the deaf.

2.Technological library needs

For example, the OPAC could have a large print capacity, or CD-ROMs could have voice-enhancement facilities.

3.Quick reference needs
This is best summarised in the words of an American student: 'It would be nice to have more people to assist us with getting books, copying articles etc. so services are available on weekends or on a drop-in basis, with less lead-time required'. [4]

The personal needs of individual students require understanding. For example, at UWE the Special Services Librarian has provided office space to a student with multiple sclerosis who gets very tired and just needs a quiet place to sit.

Arrange inductions and meetings

It is vital that the library makes effective contact with students. In addition to their attendance at regular induction programmes students will also need to learn about any special services offered to them. In fact, this kind of information should ideally be provided for prospective students, either in written form or when they come for interview. In addition to induction meetings, students can be offered meetings throughout the year. These can have various purposes. They can seek feedback from students about their use of the library, for instance about whether they have any problems, or whether a new initiative is working effectively. Meetings can also provide information to students. To an extent, library staff will have to exercise judgement about the extent to which special events or teaching should be offered to users with disabilities. Present trends in the education of disabled students are towards their complete assimilation into mainstream education. However, it is important to offer students a forum for discussion of library matters, and the goal of the librarian should be to cement a close relationship with a key group of clients.

Low cost services

The provision of new services for library users with disabilities can appear somewhat daunting because specialised equipment can be expensive. However, there is evidence from the USA that students are in fact most appreciative of low tech services. Here are a number of suggestions that have been found to work well in practice:

- it is important to use good directional signs that can be clearly read. This involves a clear font, such as Arial, and the right colours. Students with a visual impairment will most appreciate black lettering on a white or yellow background

- braille notices should be provided for the blind. These can be used not only to replicate directional signage, but also on equipment such as photocopiers. Books, articles and lectures can be provided in audio-cassette format for the blind. Volunteers can often be recruited for this task. In fact this kind of recording is best undertaken in a quiet room on campus, as a surprising amount of background noise will be present if volunteers record at home. A collection will need to be supported by the provision of an adequate number of cassette players

- videocassette programmes can have subtitles added for deaf students

- low level photocopiers are appreciated by people in wheelchairs, who may not have to ask for help if they are provided. Photocopiers that provide enlargement of text are also useful

- written guides are provided for students by most libraries. Some students will benefit from large print versions of standard library literature

- a sensible and sensitive approach to library rules and regulations is strongly recommended. For example, concessionary loans may be appropriate for certain students

- most important of all students value good levels of overall service and access to library staff. People who are ready and willing to help always come out top in any list of the library needs of students with disabilities. Getting books for students, helping with photocopying, booking facilities for people: these kinds of low tech ideas are at the heart of a good level of service.

High tech services

Although computerised equipment can be expensive, and runs the risk of becoming obsolete, it can provide real help to students who are deaf, blind or partially sighted. Deaf students will benefit from the provision of hearing loops in classrooms or around issue and enquiry desks. Equipment such as Magnilink will enlarge standard text in a variety of colours to suit individual needs. A Kurzweil machine, or other specialised combination of scanner, PC and printer will allow students to scan text into a PC and obtain either braille or voice output. The latter will be on disc for them to use at home. One user of such equipment at UWE library commented that it was the best thing since his guidedog!

Cooperate with others

In order to deliver effective services to users with disabilities a library *must* be integrated into the wider University community. These services cannot be offered effectively if the library operates in an isolated way. The library might find it useful to work with people such as the following:

Specialist staff in the Student Services department

There will usually be at least one person in a college or university who has responsibility for the interests or welfare of disabled students. The library will need to get information from this person about new intakes of students, as well as personal information about individuals, for example, which students have personal helpers. Liaison between library and other specialists can help students to spend their disability grant wisely, so that the money is not used to duplicate what is already available in the institution.

Admissions tutors in academic departments

It is vital that academic staff who are actually recruiting new students understand what services the library can and cannot provide. Lack of communication can lead to students making a decision about whether to accept a place without really knowing what support they will get once they start. It is, therefore, incumbent on the library to promote its special services to those who recruit students.

Special initiatives

Growing awareness of the need to improve institutional facilities and services for disabled staff and students has led to a number of national initiatives. One example of such initiatives is the Higher Education Funding Councils' Access to Education programme which has stimulated a whole range of projects in institutions. These projects sometimes involve developments of direct interest to the library.

External organisations

Organisations such as the RNIB and the RNID can provide useful advice to libraries. Not only that, they can sometimes allocate resources, for example by contributing to the cost of equipment. In addition, charitable organisations and local authorities sometimes offer services that libraries can subscribe to. For example, the RNIB lends books in large print as well as audio books on cassette.

Institutional policy-makers

Most important of all, the library should have effective communication with those who formulate the policies that may affect staff and students with disabilities. This may range from Estates Departments who plan and maintain buildings to those in the senior executive who allocate resources. The library needs to get its voice heard so that the planning of facilities for disabled people always recognises the role of the library in this area.

Library services to overseas students

Some UK universities are seeking to expand numbers of overseas students very considerably, to the extent of them becoming a significant proportion of the student body. They will want these students to have equality of opportunity so that they are not disadvantaged in comparison with UK students. This can only be achieved by offering them additional support. In other words, these students may not have an equal chance to succeed in UK higher education unless institutions make a real effort to help them. This applies as much to libraries as it does to academic departments.

Overseas students vary considerably. Some may be here for a term, others for several years. Some will come from western societies that share many of the cultural and social mores of UK people. Others will find almost every aspect of life strange. Yet all overseas students, including those from the USA, have in common that they are living abroad. Most of them will, therefore, feel some stress from living in a foreign country. This can affect their ability to study effectively, for example due to enhanced tiredness. Another difficulty that most overseas students have is due to the nature of UK higher education. Many students will come from educational systems that reward the memorising of facts and performance in exams. This is true not only in many Third World countries, but also in Europe and North America. They may well find the growing UK emphasis on group work, transferable skills and project work difficult to cope with. They may feel their skills are not being appreciated or rewarded. The UK expectation that students should challenge the statements of lecturers or written authorities can be unsettling for some students, as choice and freedom in selecting assignment topics and information sources can be for others. Students may expect the library to tell them where they can find the answer to a particular assignment. Yet the lecturer may expect them to do some independent research. It is clearly important that library staff should be aware of such issues.

Staff awareness

Library staff need to be made aware of issues that may affect how overseas students use the library. The University of Glasgow has an awareness programme for its staff. It is tried and tested and works well. It covers such matters as:

Communication – Speech
- pronunciation
- phonology
- grammar
- conventions.

Communication–Non-verbal

Culture
- *Culture shock.* A number of matters that appear as library problems may actually be due to cultural confusions

- *Behaviour and educational background.* For example, library staff should understand that Japanese females may consider it rude to look someone in the eye. Some males from other cultures may appear overbearing with female library staff. The purpose of awareness training is not only to identify such problems, but for staff to decide upon how to deal with such occurrences. What approach will be agreed upon to secure better understanding for both the male student and the female librarian?

Library problems

The jargon of libraries may be troublesome. Subject headings and indexes can be confusing, especially for those from cultures where surnames are not used. An understanding of alphabetical order, QWERTY and left to right order cannot always be assumed. Even the notion of *lending* books can appear strange to some students.

In addition to improving the understanding of library staff in respect of overseas students there are a number of practical steps that libraries can take:

- provide specialised library instruction. This will probably work better if more experienced students participate in such activities to act as intermediaries and to provide reassurance to their newly-arrived colleagues.

- provide a basic guide which explains how UK academic libraries operate. Such a guide would not assume any knowledge of libraries. For example, it might provide guidance about surnames. It is also useful to incorporate the library guide in any pre-arrival literature that is sent out to students by the college or university. Glasgow University library for example also produces a guide to study skills for overseas students.

- it is important to liaise regularly with those officers of the university who have particular responsibility for overseas students. This will keep the library well-informed about 'live' issues. It can also provide a platform for the library to get its messages across to students, for example by writing regularly in any bulletin or newspaper for overseas students that is produced by the institution, or by joining in social events.

Library services to part-time students

This section is concerned with those students who attend the college or university on a regular basis, such as once or twice a week. It does not address the provision of services to those who study entirely at home, as these are covered in the following section on library services to distance learners.

As has already been noted, a real difficulty facing many part-time students is lack of time. As one student has stated, 'Many of the problems such students face can be categorised in one word: 'TIME'. [5] Part-time students are likely to be working during office hours (in offices, in factories or at home as housewives). They therefore often study in short intensive sessions two or three times a week. They are often highly motivated. However, they find that their time at the college or university is filled by lectures and tutorials. Any spare time is spent in grabbing a meal, doing a spot of frantic photocopying or (most important) talking over study matters with fellow students. They tend to find that they are unable to spend enough time on vital study facilities like the library. [6]

Pressure of time has often led part-time students to identify their library as a significant obstacle to their studies. As Philip Payne has written,

> Few libraries have developed packages of services to meet their special needs. The services of most academic libraries remain stubbornly orientated towards the traditional full-time student. Part-time students are not the problem. The problem is the failure of academic libraries to adapt their services to an increasingly diverse student population.[7]

In recent years, however, a number of UK academic libraries have developed new services that discriminate in favour of part-time students. Here are some suggestions for how libraries can help part-time students to overcome the barriers to effective studying that result from shortage of time:

- opening hours can be extended in the evening so that the library is open for some time after lectures end. Weekend opening is very popular with part-time students

- collections of materials can be developed for use only by part-time students. This prevents full-time students (who have better access to the library) borrowing all the copies of a book

- a designated member of staff can take phone and fax messages from students who are unable to get to the library. This staff member can then provide advice, as well as a range of postal services

- interlibrary loan and reservations requests by part-time students can be taken by post, phone or fax, to save them a journey to the library. Books can be renewed in the same way

- articles from journals can be requested from home or work. The library then sends photocopies to the student. Likewise, books can be posted to students. In this way the library is allowing students to use the library's resources without having to be physically present

- heavily used services, such as CD-ROM databases, that are bookable can present a real problem to part-time students. Because they find it difficult to spend time in the library they are unable to compete with full-time students who can book sessions fairly easily. Library staff can offer to take bookings for part-timers by phone, again saving them time and giving them equality of opportunity

- part-time students can phone or fax to request that books be taken from the shelves and put behind the issue desk for them to collect in between classes. They save all the time it takes to search for books, and instead merely have to wait for their reserved books to be issued.

A service like that described above, which is in place in UWE library, also enables the designated member(s) of staff to form close links with part-time students (see Appendix X). The day-to-day contact, often by telephone, allows library staff to develop a very good relationship with the students, and so to attain a sound understanding of their study and library needs. This allows the special service to refer matters to other people as appropriate. It becomes a referral service. Library staff can notify academic staff of particular difficulties students encounter. This can be particularly important in a period when the growth of student numbers is reducing opportunities for contact between lecturers and students. The referral service can also alert library specialists to specific problems. For example, subject librarians may be asked to provide remedial or supplementary user education sessions in response to the discussions with students that form the core of a special service for part-time students.

Library services to distance learners

One of the greatest challenges facing academic librarians is that of providing library services to the growing numbers of distance learners. These are students who, like Open University (OU) students, very rarely, if ever, visit their college or university. They also include students who primarily study at home but who may sometimes attend their host institution for a weekend or day school or a week-long residential course. Distance learning students lack the regular contact with lecturers and libraries that part-time students have. It is already apparent that part-time students have difficulty in getting access to library services. The problems facing distance learners are even greater. Colleges and universities can emulate the OU by providing distance learning materials that are sufficient, especially if combined with a summer school and telephone access to a tutor, to enable the student to study effectively. However, few institutions have the resources to match the admirable approach of the OU. In practice distance learning courses often replicate the approach that lecturers take with full-time students, though of course without the face-to-face tutorial support. They simply do not have the resources to deploy the editorial staff, educational technologists and the other specialists that have made the OU so successful. The result is that students do not get a comprehensive package of materials and therefore they usually need to obtain further information to enable them to study effectively. Furthermore, distance learning programmes – even those offered by the OU – are not exempt from the forces of change that are currently acting upon higher education. The rise of skills-based curricula, of self-selected student projects and of independent learning affects distance learners as well as full-time and part-time students. Some recent courses demand a distinctive independent study approach from their distance learning students. The end result of all these trends is that distance learning students need to use libraries. Library research is not a luxury for the particularly keen, but a necessity for all.

But how are UK academic libraries going to meet this need? One temptation may be for libraries to ignore distance learners. The problems of supporting them can seem great and will doubtless be resource-intensive. Why not let the lecturers who design distance learning courses accept responsibility for meeting all the information needs of the students they recruit? This temptation should be resisted. Firstly, most lecturers are not able to provide students with everything they need even if they had time to do so. Secondly, in the few instances in the UK where academic departments have begun offering a postal service of books and articles to distance learners it has led to the development of new departmental collections – something most librarians will not wish to see happen. Thirdly, the students *need* access to libraries. [2] In any event, the students themselves will expect appropriate return for the fees they pay. If the library ignores their requests for support they will complain, with the consequence that the library will come to be seen as unhelpful, as a problem. It is immaterial that librarians can complain with righteous justification that the distance learning programmes should never have been set up without prior resourcing of new library services aimed at supporting them. The new courses will have financial as well as pedagogical imperatives and will doubtless match declared strategies at institutional level. Instead of complaining, academic librarians really have no choice but to face the challenge of distance learning in a spirit of positive determination. They must seek out ways of helping these students in the expectation that the parent institution is more likely to provide resources to library services that seem to be finding solutions to institutional problems, rather than to those who seem to be compounding those problems. A positive approach is essential.

Ideas for what libraries can do to support distance learners can be found in the work of a great many overseas librarians, especially in Australia and North America, as well as in the innovations of a small number of UK libraries. Of the latter, Sheffield Hallam University and Northern College, Aberdeen, are of particular interest (see Appendix XI). The following pages list some examples of practical services for distance learners from a range of UK and overseas libraries. Some of the suggestions in the previous section of this chapter for supporting part-time students are relevant also to distance learners. They can be combined with the following to provide useful services to distance learning students.

- One or more members of library staff with responsibility for supporting distance learners will be a vital prerequisite for the introduction of new services. Such a post will almost inevitably have to operate a helpline service, allowing students to make requests and enquiries by post, fax, telephone or email In the words of one US librarian, '... it is the role of the off-campus academic librarian to mediate between the high-tech world of information storage and the high-stressed world of adult learners.'

- As the student has difficulty getting to the library, the library – or at least some part of it – can go to the student. For example book boxes can be sent out to remote locations. This has long been the practice in UK Departments of Continuing Education, where tutors' visits to students have often provided the means of transportation. Alternatively, small collections can be housed within local college or public libraries, a practice that is common in North America. These collections can either be deposited for a relatively short period of time, such as a term or semester. On the other hand the cooperation of the university library with local public and college libraries can be further cemented by the joint purchasing of materials. These will be useful to local students on distance learning programmes, but will also be available to the clients of the college or public library. In such cases a clear agreement has been found to be necessary, so as to ensure that distance learners have access to materials when they need it. The American Library Association recommends that the librarian visit off-campus collections from time to time to ensure they are in good order.

- Another means of providing access to materials in the students' locality is by securing for them access to other academic libraries. The London Plus scheme is an example of this, as it allows students to borrow books from any of the university libraries participating in the scheme. See Chapter 6 for further discussion of such schemes. The benefits of the scheme extend to students at all the participating libraries. An excellent example of this approach lies in the Dutch higher education system, which gives all students the right to borrow from any academic library. Some libraries will write to other academic libraries on behalf of their distance learners so as to secure access for them. This approach can also take the form of giving students a letter of introduction to a library that is more convenient for them. A few universities even go so far as to pay any fee that is needed for their students to register to use another academic library.

- Distance learning students will need access to catalogues. The importance of catalogues has been demonstrated in numerous surveys of students. They will need a catalogue of any material that is held locally. In addition they will appreciate access to the main library catalogue. This can be provided either by depositing a microform catalogue in local centres, or by offering networked access via a modem.

- The provision of access to catalogues will go well with the supply of books, articles and even audiovisual materials by post. A growing number of UK academic libraries are supporting distance learners by means of postal services.

- Enquiry services can also be offered by post. The librarian of Northern College of Education in Aberdeen, Jean Jolly, invites students to write to her with the request '... send me something on...'. Students are given the following guidelines for making requests:

  – give as much information as possible about what you want

  – state the level of information you require, for example a simple statement of facts or a more detailed analysis

  – say if the material should be aimed for use in primary or secondary schools or with a particular age group

  – give a brief idea of what you've consulted already

  – indicate the deadline for receiving the information (see Appendix XI)

- An enquiry service for distance learners will be most effective where the library is committed to searching electronic databases on behalf of students. Sheffield Hallam University library employs a member of staff specifically to search databases on behalf of distance learners, who then receive the results by post or – exceptionally – by fax.

- By their very nature students studying at a distance will need to draw on personal attributes such as independence and self-sufficiency. However, they will study more effectively as independent learners where they receive instruction or training in study skills and information skills. Libraries that offer services to off-campus students have found a number of ways by which to teach them to study effectively and to maximise the use of whatever information sources are available to them. Here are a number of suggestions:

  - Librarians can visit the localities where students are based so as to teach them in off-campus centres.

  - Many students attend short residential courses. Librarians can ensure that information skills teaching is incorporated into these programmes.

  - Students can be invited to the main campus specifically for library teaching. Many students are keen to become effective users of libraries. One quotation from a student illustrates this point quite well: 'I managed to get into my local university library after a lot of trouble. Once in, I went straight to the section related to my course and discovered all sorts of interesting material. Then I started to browse in the journals section. I began to really feel like a student whereas before on my own at home studying the materials I couldn't really believe I was a university student. Being in the library is really important to me. I don't have much time but I try to get along after work one evening a week and sometimes on a Saturday. I'm getting more out of my course now'.[2] Such students will benefit enormously from any user education that their own university library can provide.

  - Some US libraries provide short courses for other librarians out in remote localities so that they understand better how to help their local distance learners. This could be appropriate for public librarians.

  - The University of Glasgow has a project entitled TILT, which is described in Chapter 3. TILT enables study skills tuition on computer disc to be sent to distance learners so that they can improve their ability to study by using their own PC at home. Some US librarians provide user education over the Internet.

  - Library instruction can be sent to students in the form of videocassette programmes.

- It is good practice for libraries to promote their services to client groups, and this is no less true of distance learners. A short letter of introduction to new students can help. It should be brief and friendly and explain how their library can help them. 'Working relationships can grow out of that initial letter. Telephone access, on-site visitations, correspondence and library newsletters are assertive ways of promoting and publicizing the off-campus library program.'[8] A written guide should also aim to clarify the situation for new students who may well be uncertain about what to expect. If you do post articles, but not books, both these items of information need to be clearly stated, so that students do not have false expectations.

The provision of library services to distance learners requires creativity from librarians. The problems of supporting these students are new, and so the solutions will be new. A US library contacts students via teleconferencing; a UK library provides photocopying credits to distance learners. The role of networks, e-mail and other forms of electronic communication will grow significantly in coming years. It is important that librarians keep track of developments and work out ways of supporting their own distance learning students as effectively as possible.

References

1. Tight, M. Reclaiming our traditions: part-time higher education in Britain. *Higher Education Review*, 24(2), 1992, pp.52–73.

2. Unwin, L. I'm a real student now: the importance of library access for distance learning students. *Journal of Further & Higher Education*, 18(1), 1992, pp.85–91.

3. Dequin, H.C. *et al.* The attitudes of academic librarians toward disabled persons. *Journal of Academic Librarianship*, 14(1), 1988, pp.28–31.

4. Jones, D.E. Ask, so you can give: reference and research services for the disabled in an academic library. *RQ*, 1991, 30 (4) pp479 – 485

5. Council of Polytechnic Librarians. *Part-time students: the new consumers.* Kingston: COPOL, 1988.

6. Heery, M. Improving services to part-time students in a university library. *Learning Resources Journal*, 9(1), 1993, pp.21–23.

7. Heery, M. *71 ways to help your part-time students.* Bath: Library Association University, College & Research Group, 1989.

8. Elmer, B.L. Extending library services to extended campus programs. *Rural Libraries*, 7(1), 1987, pp.63–84.

6. External cooperation

*'... every academic library should be able to identify one or more
cooperatives whose services meet its particular needs and in
which membership will significantly increase local readers' access
to information'[1]*

The case for external cooperation

Compared with countries such as Australia, the USA, and the Netherlands, UK
academic libraries do not have a strongly developed tradition of local or regional
cooperation. This may be due to the increasingly competitive nature of UK higher
education, which is a consequence of government policy. The *Follett Report* was,
for example, lukewarm about library consortia. It may be due to the ideas of
status and of hierarchies amongst academic libraries – another manifestation of a
concern with status that seems to bedevil British society. It may also be due to the
effectiveness of the British Library in supporting the majority of interlending
requirements. In countries that do not have such a well-developed centralised
national system for interlending there has long been a need for local and regional
cooperation in this field of librarianship. An important consideration, however, is
that cooperation between libraries can offer so much more than interlending.
Statewide cooperative schemes in the USA, for example, may have been initiated
to provide interlibrary loans, but now have very much wider significance. It is
our view that effective cooperation with other libraries is essential if librarians
are going to continue to meet the requirements of their users. Cooperation must
become an integral part of the management and organisation of libraries.

It is now widely recognised that academic libraries can no longer aspire to self-
sufficiency. The relentless growth in the production of academic publications is
compounded by the equally remorseless annual increase in serials prices. The
drain on budgets caused by serials collections can lead to serious imbalances in
collections whereby fewer and fewer books are bought. Even the largest libraries
can collect only a small proportion of what is relevant to their users. This is true
not only by reason of the growth of academic publishing, but also of the very
considerable growth of interdisciplinary studies. The physical presence of academic libraries has been predominant hitherto: the collections, the imposing building, the large issue desk etc. In future the physical library must be seen as a

starting point, or gateway, to information that may well be held elsewhere. The word 'library' must come to mean an information service rather than a solely physical collection. Our libraries will need to continue to build collections, but they will increasingly offer them as one element within a mix of services.

Uncertainty about the future is now common amongst academic librarians. Erens' research into research libraries has articulated the concerns of UK academic staff about the ability of library collections to support researchers.[2] Librarians are themselves equally concerned. The anxieties expressed by those with a concern for the future of UK research libraries are mirrored in similar views in the USA. However, there is in the US more of a consensus about the role of collaboration between libraries in solving the problem of inadequate collections. The US view has been well expressed by Paul Mosher:

> 'This myth of self-sufficiency has been punctuated by a set of collection ovelap studies which have covered libraries of all sizes and types. The studies demononstrate that there is a consistently large proportion of unique material distributed among libraries of a region, a state, or even a locality – whatever the mix of libraries. This conclusion is not just true of research libraries; it also applies to multi-type libraries, or small academic libraries with different sets of programs.... We have come to recognise in the US that circumstances call for cooperation in the development of collections and in their management as well–ways of optimising each library's capacity to serve its constituency with basic, core materials and to link with other libraries in partnerships or consortia that will allow access to the collectively much greater resources of all participants. We understand that cooperation permits libraries to serve their patrons and programs better, as they come to feel less collection driven and more client (and program) driven... In this new environment, most of us begin to recognize that librarians no longer need to seek the unattainable goal of self-sufficiency. We recognize that circumstances call for collaboration – distribution of responsibility in ways that will create a pattern of collaborative interdependence. This allows each library to optimize its capacity to serve its constituency with basic, core materials, and link with other libraries in consortia or networks to allow access to the collective research resources of all participants. In this framework, the unique or uncommonly held materials of each library connect with those other libraries in a pattern not unlike that of the branch libraries of a large university campus research library network. The lesser-used collections of all thus become resources for each, and the capacity to support the work of scholarship becomes greater, so long as physical and bibliographic access are adequately provided.'[3]

The impact of technological change is important because it will facilitate practical cooperation in new ways. Higginbotham and Bowdoin take a realistic approach to the impact of IT on the access and collection policies of academic libraries:

> There is something rather tedious about a library futurist; the genuine prophets and their imitators have predicted for too long what has yet to come to pass. The paperless society? Undesirable and unlikely. The printed book's death knell? Not in our lifetime, and probably not ever. Yet something new *is* coming ...access will continue to make gains over assets as a measure of the academic library's effectiveness, and new technologies will ease the transition.[1]

The case for cooperation appears overwhelming. The purpose of this chapter is to suggest practical ways by which academic librarians can provide their users with access to information beyond the walls of their own library.

Access to other academic libraries

At the simplest level of cooperation, libraries in a locality can open their doors to each other's users. In the Netherlands, for example, all students in higher education are entitled to use, and to borrow from, all higher education libraries. UK academic libraries are rather more restrictive. Some of the newer university libraries are open to the general public for reference purposes, but most libraries are fairly restrictive. As higher education has expanded rapidly, putting libraries under considerable pressure, there is an understandable reluctance to increase the number of users. Indeed, the growth of theft and vandalism in UK libraries is forcing some to adopt security measures which restrict access further. The rise of SMART card and other integrated membership/security schemes is likely to restrict access even further.

Even within some UK cooperative schemes simple access to all libraries is denied to undergraduates. The Consortium of Academic Libraries in Manchester (CALIM) is an example of a cooperative scheme that does allow free access to all libraries for all 50,000 users of those libraries. As the research effort of academic staff grows and as more students have to undertake project and dissertation work – even at undergraduate level – it is clearly beneficial to all users to have access to as wide a range of material as possible. Most collections of periodicals, statistics, official publications, law reports, encyclopaedias and directories are reference use only, so in these areas consortium users have access to materials on an equal basis to 'home' users.

Borrowing rights

A further degree of cooperation comes with the introduction of reciprocal borrowing rights, either between two libraries or for the members of a larger consortium. In the UK few consortia have gone this far for all users. However, progress can be made piecemeal. Within Avon University Libraries in Cooperation (AULIC) the three libraries of Bath, Bristol and West of England Universities provide a reciprocal borrowing scheme for all academic and research staff in the three institutions. This was then extended to research students on a trial basis, before being finalised. Reciprocal borrowing is also fairly common where institutions are adjacent to one another. For example, between Newcastle University and the University of Northumbria, and between Brighton and Sussex Universities. There are also, regrettably, a fair number of UK examples where adjacent libraries remain aloof from one another. Reciprocal borrowing also occurs where universities and further education colleges agree to franchise courses. For example, the University of Plymouth allows certain FE college students to borrow from its library.

What are the advantages of reciprocal borrowing? Obviously, it provides users with access to many more books than if they were confined to their own libraries. This simple fact is of benefit to all users, as libraries can never provide enough books to satisfy the demand. However, reciprocal borrowing also supports the educational changes that are associated with modularisation and interdisciplinary programmes. Modern trends in curriculum development in higher education promote student choice in assignments and often seek to challenge traditional subject approaches to learning by bringing together concepts and theories from a range of disciplines. The effect of cross-fertilisation between disciplines can be seen in both teaching and research, with the consequence that users require access to a wider range of library material. Indeed, opportunities for effective browsing become important in this kind of educational environment. Maurice Line agrees: ' ... users like exposure to documents. What is more, they *need* it. Many studies have shown that even in the physical sciences browsing is important; researchers pick up much valuable material in this way.' [4]

Reciprocal borrowing is also attractive as a cheaper alternative to interlibrary loans, which are expensive to process. It has other advantages. For example it may appeal to users who have a long journey to their 'host' institution. Under the terms of a cooperative scheme they can borrow books nearer home. The London Plus agreement (mentioned in Chapter 5) that was formed between London Polytechnic libraries is an example of such a scheme. The scheme has expanded since UK polytechnics became universities. As part-time and distance learning programmes proliferate any proposal that overcomes travel problems will be welcomed.

Many reciprocal borrower schemes limit the rights of external borrowers in some way. For example, it is common to limit the scheme to certain categories of borrower, or to certain times of year. Some libraries are, for instance, more cooperative in vacations than during busy term-times. It is also common for libraries to reduce the normal loan allowance for external borrowers. At UWE, for example, the allowance of fifteen items per member of staff is reduced to five for AULIC borrowers. This controls the impact of cooperative borrowing, especially at times when library stock is under pressure, yet does not diminish support for the scheme amongst users, who are generally appreciative of access to another library.

Document supply

An effective consortium will supply documents between member libraries. This is especially important where collections are being developed on a cooperative basis. In the USA the Research Libraries Group (RLG) consortium of prestigious research libraries uses the scanning, mailing and faxing of documents to provide a service to users that draws on nationwide resources. A growing number of US academic libraries participate in state-wide document delivery schemes, often involving a regular interconnecting van service. Increasingly fax and electronic document delivery are being used to speed documents between libraries.

The experience of UK libraries is different, however. Document supply schemes in higher education are few. This is largely due to the importance of the British Library Document Supply Centre (BLDSC) in supplying interlibrary loans. BLDSC has an international reputation for efficiency and cost-effectiveness. Indeed, UK consortia cannot supply documents between themselves more cheaply. This was the conclusion of the Cooperative Project East Midlands Academic Libraries, which found that '...in strict cost terms alone, given ideal circumstances, a regional scheme based on the East Midlands academic libraries would not offer any significant saving.' [5] Whether the British Library will continue to receive the funding that gives it a competitive advantage remains to be seen.

The development of electronic document delivery services has the potential to make a great impact upon cooperation between libraries. The high speed transmission of documents across networks has the power to make access policies really work. It enables libraries to move from 'just in case' to 'just in time' services. Electronic document delivery can make end-user searching effective, by supplying documents directly to the user's workstation. For example, a researcher can initiate a document request from a database of abstracts or a contents page service and receive an electronic document very quickly. Payment can be made via a credit card number. Clearly such services pose both threats and opportunities to libraries. The library is in effect being bypassed by the user going directly to the supplier of documents. The intermediary role of the librarian is removed. Indeed, such services possibly have the potential to undermine consortia of libraries, as the supply of documents commercially may become cheaper and faster than is possible from library resources.

Clifford Lynch has contemplated an interesting problem for library cooperation as a result of the growth of electronic publishing:

If a library wants to acquire material on demand it must acquire it, presumably, in many cases, from some larger library that either has not recognised the imperative to make the transition from acquiring just-in-case to just-in-time, or that has been unable to make the transition due to pressures from its user community, or that it has made a policy decision to behave like a traditional research library. This points to the development of a two-tiered system of a handful of very large, collection-oriented 'traditional' research libraries that function as service centers to smaller, more agile, acquisition-on-demand-oriented libraries. These large libraries will continue to face increasing financial pressures which will force them to charge more realistic inter-library loan costs to the more 'opportunistic' smaller libraries relying on their collections. And, as these collections become increasingly electronic, they will be unable to share more recent electronic materials limited by licence restrictions.'[6]

Whether Lynch's vision will materialise remains to be seen. However, it is presumably within the power of publishers to recognise this possibility, and to support the access model in libraries, and to adjust their charging policies accordingly.

However, electronic document delivery may also offer opportunities for inter-library cooperation. The role of librarian *vis-à-vis* the end-user may be strengthened by means of effective sponsorship, promotion and training of end-users in the efficient use of electronic document retrieval. The development of inter-institutional networking, for example in metropolitan area networks, offers opportunities for the fast transfer of electronic documents between cooperating libraries. The use of the Ariel software by six academic libraries in California shows that it can be quick and effective to scan documents in one library, transmit them across the academic network and laser print them in the recipient library. The *Follett Report* identifies both subject-based consortia and regional consortia being helped by developments in electronic document delivery.

Electronic document delivery and the related development of electronic publishing, such as e-journals, are subject to both technical and copyright problems that make practical progress lag well behind some of the optimistic ideas expressed in the professional literature. However, progress *is* being made and cooperation between libraries will develop as a result.

Collection development

Cooperative collection development is one of the most important challenges facing academic librarians. It is fraught with difficulties, yet progress must be made. Its rationale is clear. Changing methods of teaching and learning lead to students doing more projects and dissertation work, which in turn requires them to undertake more and more library research. They need access to more and more sources of information. At the same time the research effort of universities is growing and the information needs of researchers are becoming more demanding. Yet library budgets are declining, a situation compounded by steadily increasing serials prices and the exponential growth in academic publishing. The result is that collections are really struggling to meet the demands being placed upon them. Librarians must act if they are to avoid incurring real criticism and a significant loss of support from their users. It is widely recognised that academic libraries are increasingly unable to satisfy the needs of their users from within their own collections. It therefore is essential that effective access policies are implemented, so that the library is able to draw on resources that are held elsewhere. Current interlibrary loan practices are obviously relevant to the problem, and most academic libraries are struggling to satisfy the demand for interlibrary loans. The scale of the problem is such that other, newer solutions must be found. Much is said and written of the power of electronic publishing and IT networking to provide the solution. In the longer term this may well be the case. However, the electronic library is bedevilled by problems that prevent it making anything but gradual and piecemeal progress. IT developments will make an impact over time and it is important that librarians encourage relevant research and other initiatives. The problem, however, exists in the here and now. It is not advisable for librarians to wait and hope for an electronic solution to be provided for them. Positive action is needed now.

Cooperative collection development backed by document delivery and reciprocal borrowing is attractive because it allows meagre resources to be deployed more cost effectively. Libraries cease trying to do the impossible, i.e. buy everything, and instead they agree to share resources in a planned way. Core collections continue to be built up at each institution, but the wider requirements, for example of researchers, are met from the collective resources of the consortium. The idea is a simple one, but seems to be difficult to achieve in practice. What practical steps can be taken to encourage and to implement cooperative collection development?

- First, and perhaps most important of all, librarians need to adopt a positive attitude to cooperation. Smith and Johnson express this idea as follows:

  If research librarians are to reconfigure their programs they must make some major changes in how their libraries operate. They must certainly change their posture toward interlibrary borrowing and lending, which must be transformed from a last resort to a primary activity. They must move their resource-sharing operations out of the nooks and crannies in which they are all-too-frequently lodged and provide them with sufficient support so that they can become a viable alternative to on-site collections. Interlibrary loan deserves not only a change of name but a face-lift and a new personality. It must be overhauled, expanded and moved front and center within research library facilities, priorities and budgets. It must be staffed with some of the library's most effective, most service minded personnel.[7]

The force of this statement, and of the degree of change being advocated, is brought home by contemplating the obscure physical location and the 'backroom' nature of many interlibrary loan offices.

- A change of attitude also means a reversal of the insularity of some academic librarians. It is often overlooked that the professionally active staff who build up personal networks of contacts in other libraries may not be representative of the profession. Yet successful cooperative development depends upon librarians who are committed to developing professional relationships. They need to be flexible, and able to negotiate and to compromise with others. They need to understand the position of others in the consortium. They do not need the competitive attitude of mind which equates size of collection to professional status, and which is too concerned about status to build professional relationships of trust and friendly cooperation.

- Effective collaboration is likely to occur where the consortium sets up small teams of staff from different libraries. For example, teams can be responsible for reviewing and developing collections in specific subject areas. Teams are also a very effective means of developing specific initiatives. They foster understanding and a cooperative spirit within staff. It is from a sense of identification with one another and of each other's professional objectives that concrete progress develops. Teams need to meet regularly, so that cooperative activities become built into working life. Cooperation between libraries sometimes founders on the need to recover common ground at meetings that are too infrequent and appear somewhat removed from day to day work.

- It is incumbent on librarians to try to persuade their researchers and other users of the need to support an access policy rather than a holdings policy. A positive attitude to cooperation is not just something that concerns our dealing with like-minded librarians. It requires persistent and vigorous promotion within the institution's academic community. Librarians should take issue with the attitudes of researchers. 'In what has been described as the 'law of least effort' patrons usually place convenience of access well before the quality of resource. Such behaviour may run afoul of cooperative efforts, which by definition involve a trade-off of some immediate support to local users in order to contribute materials in support of an extended network of users.' [8] Cooperative schemes need the backing of the institutions as well as their libraries. There is clearly a role for librarians to provide energy and leadership in winning institutional support and resources for cooperative activities such as collection development.

- Effective collection development needs to be properly planned. Cooperation needs to be guided by properly thought out objectives, structures and
guidelines. An excellent example of this is the RLG Conspectus Programme.
This provides a clear framework within which libraries map out the strengths
of their collections in an agreed format that collectively provides a national
overview of research collections. It is a method of planning collection development that is transferable to any local or regional group of libraries. It
has, for example, been used by a group of Scottish academic libraries. In a
number of US consortia cooperation over collection development takes the
form of a collective financial plan for acquisitions. Budgets are allocated
in support of the collective acquisitions policy. For example, the Network
of Alabama Academic Libraries (NAAL) uses a formula for the spending
of acquisitions funds in agreed subject areas. [9] It uses the following guidelines in its collection development programme:

    - strength of each collection in relation to available materials
    - strength of each collection in relation to other collections on
      the same subject
    - deficiencies and gaps in coverage within statewide resources
    - current and anticipated demands of the graduate programme
      supported by the collection
    - unique collections and resources
    - institutional resources available to maintain and strengthen the
      collection.

The scale of the scheme requires a detailed planning process that contrasts with the
informal nature of much cooperation between academic libraries. However, the commitment is felt to be justified by '... the need to acquire research materials for Alabama that would lie beyond the capability of any one institution.' The scheme has
provided tangible benefits (e.g. funding) for collection development precisely because of its large-scale, planned approach that is seen as being of real benefit to higher
education across the state. There is no reason why such developments should not take
place within UK regions, if the will is present within cooperating institutions.

- Research has shown that as many as 50% of the volumes in a large research
collection may never be used, and that 20% of the collection may account
for 80% of use.[8] Concern about acquisitions policies and budgetary management is understandable. However, a formal programme of collection
development within a consortium will enhance the collection management
skills of the participating librarians. Ability to evaluate collections will
improve as more control is brought to an area of librarianship that is some-

times prone to 'intuitive' purchasing. A cooperative collection development programme will need to be planned, developed and monitored in a consultative way that inevitably requires careful reflection about the use of acquisitions funds.

- In the USA state-wide schemes that are widely perceived as effective have acted to protect library budgets. This is because eligibility for participation in the attractive collection development programme requires that contributing libraries can play a full part. This has, therefore, acted as a brake on institutions which have considered cutting library funding. They have not done so because it would jeopardise membership of the state scheme. Librarians may, therefore, be strengthened financially and politically by participating in an effective programme of cooperative collection development.

Staff development and training

Consortia of libraries that are based within a locality can significantly enhance training and development opportunities for library staff. The quality and range of what is available to library staffs within a consortium can be improved in a cost-effective manner. A starting point for such a development will be the creation of a committee or group of staff that have responsibility for continuing professional development (CPD) in member libraries. For example, CALIM has a Staff Training and Development Working Party which has the remit: 'To consider and to implement policies and programmes designed to address key issues of training, development and job satisfaction of all levels of staff in CALIM libraries'[10] The CALIM scheme also benefits from the joint funding of a development officer who works full-time on CALIM matters, and who plays a particularly important part in CPD activities within and across the five member libraries. More informal links between the staff development programmes of libraries can also be effective, if individuals are sufficiently well-motivated to make things happen. A cooperative approach to training and staff development can have the following results:

- creation of a regular programme of workshops and seminars
- opportunities and funding to bring in professional trainers who may be beyond the resources of individual libraries
- savings from joint training activities. The CALIM scheme has established a collective training fund of c. £9,000 and reckons to save c. £60,000 on the costs which would have been incurred had each library made its own arrangements and sent staff to outside training events.[10]
- exchange of information about each library's staff development programme. The exchange can lead to the spread of good practice and of imaginative ideas from one library to another

- an audit of staff expertise can be undertaken. The sharing of expertise can follow, enriching individual training programmes
- opportunities for formal training can be increased, for example for Library Association registration and chartership
- visits of staff to other libraries can be encouraged. This may take the form of group visits, or of individual visits, both of which can remove prejudices and increase understanding
- shadowing schemes can be set up whereby staff spend a day or a week with someone doing a similar job in another library within the consortium. Similarly, exchanges of staff can be encouraged. Appendix XII shows the guideline for the staff exchange and work shadowing scheme adopted by AULIC consortium
- printed bulletins, e-mail groups and lists can be set up to publicise training activities and to foster regular communication.

Cooperation over training and staff development is useful because it is relatively easy to organise. The consortium can make progress in this area because its resources are wholly under the control of the member libraries. It does not require negotiation with users or institutional managers. It is also an area that is not threatening to traditional practices. Even where library staff have some resistance to change, joint staff development activities are self-evidently sensible and are not disruptive. Yet they can be an ideal means by which people get to know each other, barriers can be broken down and a true spirit of cooperation be fostered.

Collaborative negotiating

Consortia of libraries can often negotiate with library suppliers more effectively than individual libraries. This is a long-standing form of cooperation that can embrace the purchase of furniture, shelving and workstations as much as periodicals subscriptions. The development of new electronic sources of information has stimulated new ways by which libraries exercise their negotiating skills. For example, consortia of libraries can negotiate for discounts on CD-ROMs and other databases from suppliers who are keen to sell to the member libraries. For example, the M25 Consortium of academic libraries in London has ' ... held negotiations with serials and CD-ROM agents and produced documentation to inform decision making. Suppliers offer discounts relating to the volume of business from M25 members; and members are more aware of what types of overall deals they can receive from suppliers. An electronic table of contents (Etoc) demonstration day was held for M25 staff at South Bank University, and a Databases Group has been investigating consortium deals for online periodical indexes. The aim would be to get a reasonable deal for an Etoc with the subscriptions held by M25 members highlighted in some way.'[11] It will be apparent from this example, which is increasingly typical, that a consortium of libraries can provide cost-effective solutions to the problems facing most academic libraries. Not only are services in individual libraries enhanced by a development such as Etoc, but the consortium is itself strengthened. The member libraries have a reason for increasing their commitment to the consortium and this in turn facilitates the development of new, consortium-wide services. For example, databases can be networked across all member libraries, offering information about all local holdings. The consortium can therefore enhance the usefulness of services such as Blackwell's Uncover by adding local information to its bibliographical entries. In this way the services themselves can become more useful to library users.

Individual cooperation

This chapter has so far covered cooperation between libraries. However, the importance of links between individual librarians cannot be overemphasised. In some ways the links between individuals form the basic building blocks of larger cooperative schemes. They are also an important means whereby librarians keep themselves informed about professional matters. Everyone can learn from visits to and conversations with professional colleagues in other institutions.

There are many examples of professional groupings that facilitate updating and exchange of good practice. Professional associations such as Aslib, SCONUL and the Library Association are obviously very important. So too are the subgroups that cater at national level for more specialised needs. For example, the Library Association's COFHE group brings together librarians in further and higher education. SCONUL has subject groupings that offer training and development to librarians who work in broad subject areas such as the humanities and science and technology. Independent bodies like the British and Irish Association of Law Librarians and the British Business Schools Librarians Group perform a similar function. Above all, groups such as these allow librarians to learn from each other and to get inspiration and help in solving day-to-day work problems.

Academic librarians worth their salt will also build networks across the invisible boundaries that sometimes seem to surround higher education. For example an engineering subject librarian will benefit enormously from making contact with engineering librarians working in local special libraries. A law librarian will benefit from good links with librarians in local law firms, and so on. The benefits derived can include:

- exchanges of information and good practice with fellow professionals

- an understanding for academic librarians of practical librarianship in a corporate and professional environment. This is particularly useful in guiding

the user education programmes of students who will leave university to
work with professional and corporate information sources

- the formation of an overview of local information resources to which students and academic staff can be directed

- cooperation over stock, whereby reports and other literature can be provided free, or where superseded editions of reference works can be acquired

- opportunities for joint training activities, for visits and for the placement of trainees, in just the same way as applies to consortia of academic libraries.

It is perhaps worth noting that as academic libraries move from policies of collection holding to policies of access to information they will increasingly resemble special libraries. Commercial, industrial, professional and governmental libraries have long operated access policies. They have often been in the forefront of library automation and in the use of electronic information sources. If the electronic library exists it is most likely to be found in the kind of libraries described by Michel Bauwens[12] who advocates highly automated information services within large corporations that are run by individuals based in divisional teams rather than in libraries. He uses the term 'cybrarian' to describe these individuals, who have relinquished all use of paper-based collections. Bauwens' views are somewhat futuristic. However, electronic library services are well advanced in some corporations. Academic librarians can learn a lot from the experience of special librarians. This is likely to become more true as time passes.

Links between further and higher education libraries

Another important link is that which exists between libraries in the further and higher education sectors. Such links may be the informal but useful type of cooperation that occurs between academic and special libraries. However, more formal links have developed in the UK in recent years as a result of the franchising of HE level courses in FE institutions. University courses may be run in colleges in their entirety, which often happens with sub-degree level courses. Alternatively, only part of a course may run in a local college. Typically this will be the first year of a degree programme. Where franchising occurs the relationship between the libraries of the two institutions is almost certain to arise as an issue.

Decisions will need to be made about such matters as:

- is the college library able to support the franchised HE level course?

- what is the role of the university library in assessing the college library?

- what guidelines exist for making such an assessment?

- what start-up resources are available for the college library?

- what mechanisms are there for evaluating the continuing ability of the college library to support the course?

- should the University library offer borrowing rights to college staff and students, or should the University insist that the college library support the franchised course wholly from its own resources?

The process of franchising courses should involve university librarians in considerable contact with their colleagues in the colleges. This contact can be both formal and informal. The questions posed above require that the librarians – in conjunction with other institutional managers – formulate policies that define the nature of their relationship. This may well change over time, as the relationship is cemented at institutional level, or as understanding grows about the needs of staff and students in both university and college. For example, at UWE borrowing rights were not offered to staff or students in franchise colleges in the first instance. This is because it was decided that college resources should be the only source of support to college libraries. However, over time the university developed close working relationships with college staff teaching on franchised courses. Library borrowing rights were offered to these staff in recognition of their staff development needs. In the same way, borrowing rights were extended to college students on courses which began in colleges but transferred into the later years of UWE courses. This was properly funded, and recognised the institutional need to inculcate a sense of identity with the university in such college students. They would, for example, often visit faculties and have an introduction to the university library while still in their first year of study at the college.

Deborah Goodall has conducted interesting research into the nature of the links between college and university libraries. [13] She found that whilst some universities offered no support to colleges, some universities did offer a range of services. These include:

- borrowing rights for staff

- borrowing rights for students

- free interlibrary loans

- reduced rate interlibrary loans

- free photocopying for example of journal articles to add to college library stock

- reduced rate photocopying

- computer link to university library catalogue

- microfiche copy of university library catalogue

- CD-ROM copy of university library catalogue

- advice from subject librarians

- regular updating of reading lists.

Where links are to be strong and healthy there will have to be informal and face-to-face contact between librarians in the colleges and in the university. Goodall has found that such links can vary from non-existent to 'difficult and patchy' to 'very helpful'. 'Positive comments focused on staff development, professional contacts, networking, and achieving a raised profile within the university.' Goodall concludes by noting that overall more effort seems to be put into making franchising work by the college librarians than by their colleagues in higher education libraries.

Links between universities and colleges are still changing. UK further education is undergoing considerable development since incorporation. This can be seen, for example, in the creation of large metropolitan tertiary colleges through the merger of several FE colleges. Some UK universities are pursuing regional strategies that designate certain colleges as 'associate' or 'affiliated' institutions. There may well be further alliances of this sort in the future. Opportunities for making FE–HE links closer may arise out of the educational and technological changes sweeping through all institutions. The spread of open and distance learning causes educational problems that are similar in both sectors. Likewise, both HE and FE institutions must grapple with the incorporation of computer-assisted learning, databases, PCs and the Internet into teaching and learning. Regional networks offer opportunities for mutual support and the sharing of experience. This is as true for libraries as it is for teaching methods. Large libraries could have a growing role in supporting the IT infrastructure and information networking of colleges. In other words they can act as the hub of network of academic libraries within a region. In turn college libraries can form part of a regional web that supports the university's part-time and distance learning students. Whatever the future, cooperation between librarians in these two sectors of education is likely to grow.

Conclusion

This chapter has indicated some ways by which academic libraries can work together to solve common problems and to enhance services to their users. External cooperation is an area which highlights very well both the forces acting upon academic libraries and the nature of the developments that libraries must undertake. Technological change combined with growing financial pressures and users' seemingly insatiable demands for information together form a formidable imperative for change. The very nature of the academic library is having to change, as traditional approaches to collection building become unsustainable. The modern academic library must develop focused collection management policies which will support the specific needs of current teaching, learning and research programmes. Alongside this will be services that offer users access to the vast sources of information that exist outside the library. The library's links with the world outside the home institution are clearly going to grow and grow in importance. Whatever the technology employed to achieve contact with the external world it is apparent that successful access policies will rely upon a strong service orientation in libraries. The library must be organised to work very closely with users, to understand their information needs and to find ways of delivering appropriate information to them from across the globe. User satisfaction, rather than the size of collection, must become the primary means of evaluating an academic library. The right formula for successful external cooperation would appear to bring together collection management skills, the ability to harness and exploit the opportunities that arise from technology and a strong commitment to high levels of service to users. Expressed in this way, it is clear that successful external cooperation, like the successful implementation of change in academic libraries, leads us to consider the skills and abilities that are required of academic librarians. The skills needed by the modern academicli brarian are the subject of the next chapter.

References

1.   Higginbotham, B.B and Bowdoin, S. *Access versus assets: a comprehensive guide to resource sharing for academic librarians*. Chicago: American Library Association, 1993.

2.   Erens, R. *Research libraries in transition*. Library and Information Research Report 82. London: British Library, 1991.

3.   Mosher, P. Collaborative collection development in an era of financial limitations. *Australian Academic and Research Libraries*, 20(1), 1989, pp.5–15.

4.   Line, M. Access as a substitute for holdings: false ideal or costly reality. *Interlending & Document Supply,* 23(2), 1995, pp.28–30.

5.   MacDougall, A.F. Academic library cooperation and document supply: possibilities and considerations of cost-effectiveness. *Journal of Librarianship*, 21(2), pp.186–189.

6.   Lynch, C.A. The transformation of scholarly communication and the role of the library in the age of networked information. *Serials Librarian*, 23(3/4), 1993, pp.14.

7.   Smith, E. and Johnson, P. How to survive the present while preparing for the future: a research library strategy. *College and Research Libraries*, 54(5), 1993, pp.389–396.

8.   Bril, P. Cooperative collection development: progress from apotheosis to reality. in Jenkins, C. and Morley, M., eds. *Collection management in academic libraries*. Aldershot: Gower, 1991, pp.235–258.

9.   Medina, S.O. The evolution of cooperative collection development in Alabama academic libraries. *College & Research Libraries,* 53(1), 1992, pp.7–19.

10.   Harris, C. Resource sharing:the CALIM experience.*Taking Stock,* 4(1) , 1992, pp.8–11.

11.   Dolphin, P. A driving force within the M25. *Library Association Record,* 97(10), October 1995, p.541.

12.   Bauwens, M. The emergence of the 'cybrarian': a new organisational model for corporate libraries. *Business Information Review,* 9(4), 1993, pp.65–67.

13.   Goodall, D. Franchising courses, library resources: the view from both sides. *Library and Information Research News*, 18(61), Winter 1994, pp.22–28.

7. Developing skills for the future

'The rapid developments in computer technology as well as economic changes have made it clear that the familiar role of librarians as information intermediaries must undergo immense change if librarians are to avoid being displaced by a variety of contenders'[1]

Speculation on what the library of the future will look like has become increasingly popular. The issue has been explored not only in the professional literature but also through regular electronic discussion lists and bulletin boards. [2] The question also continues to intrigue those conducting job interviews in academic librarianship. Of course, such forecasting is partly dependent on the timescale envisaged but can cover a number of different scenarios. These range from the idea of information technology retaining its role in support of printed texts for many years to come through to the library as a physical entity disappearing completely. In this scenario the library becomes almost independent of time and place. Although similar discussions have taken place in the past in relation to microform formats and the early experiments with automation, recently this issue has acquired a more urgent and focused edge. Rapid technological developments are taking place in a number of areas, in particular global networking and telecommunications, digitisation and electronic publishing and delivery. These are acting as catalysts in focusing the attention of information professionals, the academic community and, thanks to the interest shown by the mass media, the general public. The virtual library, the library without walls and the electronic campus are just some of the terms regularly used to conceptualise the library of the future. A more cautious note is struck by Stoll who warns against the danger of a 'library without value' rather than without walls. [3]

Perhaps inevitably, some librarians cling to the idea of an academic library as a great collection proudly tended by scholar-librarians. Fred Ratcliffe articulates such nostalgia in his romantic notions of work in the research library: 'The centre of intellectual life among librarians was traditionally in the cataloguing room, among those engaged in the production of the main bibliographical tool in the library ... cataloguing and classifying in a great academic library is intellectually demanding. It requires intellectual stamina and a disciplined mind'[4] The self-sufficiency and security of the cataloguing room belong to a bygone age. The professional skills that have sustained the research libraries in the past will have to change radically.

Inevitably, the discussion then turns to the future role of the academic librarian in this envisaged world of technological and educational sophistication. How will our role change? What new skills will be needed? Which of the librarian's traditional skills will be retained? How will the convergence of support services affect staffing structures, responsibilities and working conditions? What effect will unemployment and increased competition for jobs have on the types of skill requirements? Will the librarian as a species disappear alongside the library as a physical entity?

Core skills

In Chapter 1 we emphasised the plurality of information formats – the electronic sitting alongside the printed. It is difficult and possibly futile to be more precise about the likely balance between the two. This is the premise on which this chapter's discussions are based. However, only one set of skills highlighted here is related to information technology. Important though such skills are and will be in the future, there is a danger that people- and service-based skills will become neglected, particularly in the professional literature. There is a certain irony here. The more the debate revolves around information technology, the greater the realisation that it is the people – the various constituents within the academic community – who are the significant players. Information technology will continue to be the means rather than the end. In our view helping to connect people with the required information regardless of format will remain a basic tenet of academic librarianship. Information technology will continue to develop and represent one vehicle among many through which this connectivity will be achieved. The time when students and academic staff interact regularly and effectively with library and information services without the need for guidance and advice is a long way off.

Periodically, there is a debate about the best model to provide library and information services within further and higher education. Unlike Heseltine [5], we reject the suggested demise of subject librarianship. Currently, it remains the model most suited to the provision of support for teaching, learning and research. It is through this subject-based approach that the services outlined in the preceding chapters are delivered most effectively. It is the best available option for integrating the work of libraries into the educational process. This view is also supported by the *Fielden Report*, the *Ross Report* [6] and House and Moon. [7]

Before turning to the particular skills required for the future, it needs to be stressed that there are key areas of traditional information work where proficiency is still required. These will apply to any librarian or information professional regardless of the sector in which he or she operates. These are some of them:

- identifying and meeting the information needs of the clientele
- identifying, accessing, organising, interpreting and evaluating knowledge and information
- interpersonal and communication skills
- professional development including updating IT-related skills
- generic management skills.

This final chapter highlights some of the core skills which we believe are essential for the academic librarian of today and the foreseeable future. The skills and qualities are grouped under the following headings:

- credibility with academic staff
- teaching and training
- IT-related skills
- management skills.

Credibility with academic staff

The importance of institutional (Chapter 1) and departmental (Chapter 2) integration to offering an effective service has already been highlighted. A wide range of practical activities and particularly advice on participating in meetings has been offered in order to help achieve success. We believe that it is essential for the librarian to gain credibility in an educational role and that this represents the key to effective integration. There are few quick and easy ways of developing these skills and attitudes. How to achieve credibility with academic staff is difficult to describe. However, rather like politicians possessing that quality of gravitas, it is immediately recognisable when you come across it. Hidden behind the notion of 'credibility' is a variety of elements including status, academic qualifications, subject-based knowledge, academic activities, personal qualities and professionalism. These are important enough to warrant further discussion.

Status

The status of the librarian within the faculty or department has been a continuing source of debate in the USA.[8-10] Resolution appears no nearer as librarians strive to reach a consensus on two issues:

- are librarians' responsibilities suitably scholarly, academic and professional to qualify as faculty?
- should librarians have similar conditions of service and performance criteria as academic staff?

In the UK professional literature less prominence is given to the librarian's formal status within institutions. There is, however, a wide variety of different perceptions on the librarians role within the academic community. Are they administrators, educators, some kind of hybrid, providers of support, scholars, professionals or merely curators who stamp books? The perceptions of academic staff can be reinforced or altered in a number of ways:

- improving the standing of the library service within the institution generally raises the standing of the librarians as individual professionals

- the librarian who has confidence in the library's role in relation to academic departments is able to speak convincingly about meeting their information needs

- librarian visibility within academic departments is an important source of awareness raising. This may include participating in and presenting papers at influential meetings. It can take the form of participating confidently in academic discussions about teaching, learning and research. It may also take in more subtle activities such as e-mailing staff for their opinions, involvement in social events or organising departmental workshops

- it is unhelpful for those librarians who are highly paid and whose conditions of service may resemble their academic counterparts to be seen carrying out tasks which are inappropriate for that level of staff. It may also be inadvisable on purely economic grounds.

Basically, the academic librarian is seeking parity of esteem within a community of scholars.

Academic qualifications and subject knowledge

The librarian who has a graduate or postgraduate qualification in a subject relevant to a particular department or faculty will gain credibility by virtue of subject familiarity. Where there are no formal subject qualifications, a broad knowledge of the areas covered by the departments is usually a prerequisite for dealing with ease with the academic staff. A higher degree obtained in library and information studies demonstrates an affinity not only with postgraduate students and their problems of studying at that level but also with the academic staff many of whom will have a similar level of qualification. Increasingly, academic librarians are recognising the importance of their educational role by gaining teaching qualifications.

Academic activities

To be able to participate in scholarly activities undoubtedly increases the librarian's credibility. This may take the form of:

- publishing journal articles, books, chapters etc
- editorships
- presenting papers at or organising conferences

As referred to briefly in Chapter 2 there is also a variety of institutional activities in which librarians can take part – to the benefit of the institution, the department, the library and the individual. These may include visits from validating bodies, inspections by Government officials, teaching and research assessments, institutional reviews or representation on cross-departmental bodies. The effect which the librarian's contribution to such high-profile events has on other academic staff should not be underestimated.

Personal qualities

The librarian who is positive, proactive, highly motivated and assertive is likely to foster productive relationships with academic staff and give them confidence in his or her ability. The effective librarian will not let him-or herself be intimidated. The library profession has an obsession with its own image which is partly self-generated but also fuelled by the mass media. Although the problem is less pronounced in academic libraries, there still remains a hard core of perceptions which include lack of confidence, modesty, resistance to change, inferiority and introversion. Employers and library schools have a responsibility to ensure that entrants to the profession possess the appropriate personal qualities. When such qualities are accompanied by effective interpersonal skills – in particular, communication skills – credibility is enhanced.

Professionalism

Librarians who demonstrate a 'professional' approach to their work gain the respect of academic colleagues and users alike. This professional/client relationship may work at an informal level, for example by ensuring that agreed action resulting from a enquiry is actually followed up. At a more formal level it can take the form of an appointments or surgery system. This system, which is referred to in Chapter 4, demonstrates the value of the librarian's time and has parallels with common practice in other professions such as solicitors, doctors and dentists.

Teaching and training

We believe that the librarian's educational role forms the central plank on which his or her other duties and responsibilities are built. This approach is recognised by the Fielden Report: 'Subject librarians will have to understand teaching/learning skills if they begin to fulfil para-academic functions'. [11]

The importance we attach to ensuring that students become self-reliant information users is reflected in the coverage of this issue in Chapter 3. Inculcating these skills will remain the key focus of the academic librarian for the foreseeable future.

In addition to the core skills required for providing effective user education, it is apparent that the librarian needs to become more adaptable and flexible in the teaching and learning environment. Increasingly there are encouraging examples in which the librarian (in conjunction with academic staff) has the freedom to organise the structure, methods, location and evaluation of programmes. All too often in the past, much of the programme detail has been imposed by others. The ability to take either of these scenarios and turn it into an experience which benefits the student requires flexibility and adaptability.

So what elements does the librarian have to take into account?

The librarian needs to:

- be equally comfortable whether user education takes place with one person or with a large group

- be equally comfortable whether the session takes place in an informal but familiar setting (a tutorial in the librarian's office) or in a formal but unfamiliar one (a room within the academic department with minimal equipment)

- understand how students or organise their studies and how they go about learning. In this way library programmes may be tailored to majority needs and styles of learning

- become familiar with a wide variety of teaching and learning methods including coaching, facilitation, workbooks, joint or group teaching and, increasingly nowadays, the opportunities provided by the electronic classroom

- be aware of different types of users and not just those covered in Chapter 5. These include those students coming directly from schools, tertiary and further education colleges, higher education colleges, universities, mature students, women returners etc

- aim to turn constraints – staffing, time, size of group, facilities – into opportunities where negotiations have proved unsuccessful

- build into user education programmes appropriate provision for short- and long-term skills acquisition

- be prepared to innovate and take risks whenever the opportunity presents itself

- be able to apply his or her pedagogical skills and knowledge to each of the components of the *Fielden Report's* matrix of learner support. (This can be found on page 25 of the *Report*.)

- become involved, where appropriate, in helping academic staff to design and develop course material. This may be particularly helpful where open and distance learning operate
- become involved in wider study skills programmes.

As we shall see in the following section, IT-related skills will continue to be highly prized assets in the coming years. To transfer some of these skills successfully from librarians to ever increasing numbers of students is a formidable challenge.

IT-related skills

It is information technology which generates the most vigorous debate in relation to the changing role of the librarian. Technological advances continue to ask questions of the support services, including the library. Library services – whether converged or not – are examining their policies on the balance between collection development and the accessing of information electronically. Most academic libraries have some degree of involvement in this latter process either through more traditional interlibrary loan services or via more sophisticated document delivery.

The importance of information technology to the modern academic library has been recognised throughout the preceding chapters. The breadth of changes associated with technological development is very well illustrated in the UK Electronic Libraries Programme (eLib) which was spawned by the *Follett Report*. The projects within eLib demonstrate the pervasive nature of the changes likely to take place in academic libraries. The programme has considerable relevance to the way in which libraries are organised. This can be seen, for example, in the impact of electronic document delivery on cooperation between libraries, an issue which is considered in Chapter 6. Indeed, the eLib programme itself has stimulated cooperation within the library community, as many bids for funding were consortium-based.

The Electronic Libraries Programme represents an ambitious attempt to deal with technological change in a positive, proactive way. For example, the aims of the programme address the publishing environment of libraries as well as academic libraries themselves.

There are six programme areas within eLib:

- electronic document and article delivery
- electronic journals
- digitisation
- on demand publishing

- training and awareness
- access to network resources.

In addition there are some supporting studies. Further information about the specific projects within eLib can be obtained via the UK Office of Library Networking (UKOLN) at *http:// ukoln.bath.ac.uk/elib/*.

The eLib projects include SEREN, a geographically based document delivery service by a consortium of academic libraries in Wales; Netskills which aims to provide a comprehensive national network skills training programme; *Internet Archaeology*, which will take the form of a new electronic journal; Phoenix, a project which is concerned with the implementation of electronic storage and print techniques to supply texts to students; ADAM, which will develop a UK-based information server giving access to Art, Architecture, Design and Media resources; and an Internet library of 18th and 19th century journals. These examples provide an indication of the range of projects. All of these point towards a significant change in the services offered by libraries, and of the skills required by librarians. The projects point toward a period in UK academia of very considerable staff development and training if new IT-based services are to be effective.

IT-related skills and competences are discussed under two headings:

- tailored navigational support
- IT management

Tailored navigational support

This term was coined in the Follett Committee's supplementary report on IT [12]. This continually evolving set of skills, which is in complete contrast to the custodial role of the past, implies that the librarian:

- keeps up-to-date with subject-based knowledge and accompanying IT developments
- has an advisory role in guiding students and staff through the diverse range of electronic sources and formats
- is fully conversant with sometimes highly sophisticated search methods
- has the necessary skills to train library staff and users

These navigational support skills work on two levels – the operational and the strategic.

Operational
At the operational level the librarian requires the skills to gain access to electronic sources of information including knowledge of licenses, protocols, modems, interfaces etc. This role is sometimes termed access engineer. Having gained

access to a source, the ability to find one's way to the required information efficiently and effectively is vital. The diversity of software and charging formats makes this particularly difficult. The librarian has to demonstrate a consistent level of competence whether searching a CD-ROM database, accessing an expensive online service or making hypertextual links across cyberspace. Naturally, communication and training skills, including those covered in Chapter 3, are essential to transfer the operational competences to others. A particularly sensitive approach is required when training technophobics. For the librarian who makes only intermittent use of certain electronic services it is advisable to ensure that a personal or organisation skills updating programme operates. If in the short term this is impractical, designating individual librarians as 'experts' in particular electronic services is one way forward.

Strategic

The navigational support provided at the strategic level requires the application of critical, evaluative and interpretative skills. The diverse range of sources available to the librarian or user means that decisions have to be made about which are best suited to meet the information needs. As House and Moon rightly point out:

> The key contribution of the subject librarian may well be not simply the tracking down of a wider and wider range of less and less useful information, but the interpretation of the likely value of that information to potential users. [7]

The librarian's knowledge, experience and skills are all important in offering advice and guidance on the appropriateness of sources. For example, decisions have to be made between printed and electronic, between online and CD-ROM, between CD-ROM and Internet sources, between different sources on the Internet, between indexing, abstracting and full-text services. This resembles more the role of information or knowledge manager, part of whose remit is to facilitate the productive use of the virtual library.

The importance of acquiring these navigational skills has been recognised and is reflected not only in the welcome eLib programme but also in university departments of information studies. An example of current trends is given by Hodges: 'Trainee librarians of today have to know how to use the machine, and how to interrogate the system through the machine, but the important thing is which information is useful to the individual being helped.' [13]

The information technology elements of most library school curricula have expanded enormously. It is important that this trend continues so that the right calibre of librarian possessing skills appropriate to current and future academic libraries feeds the profession.

The eLib Programme has established a number of projects which have particular relevance to the acquisition of navigational skills. Under the heading of Training and Awareness are two projects which merit further discussion – Netskills and ARIADNE. Under the heading of Access to Network Resources are projects which aim to provide gateways to subject-based Internet resources. These are enormously helpful in distilling and filtering quality sources. The Social Science Information Gateway (SOSIG) is one particularly good example.

Netskills

The University of Newcastle is the lead institution which is providing a programme of training and awareness for academic users of information and those supporting them. Training will be provided covering the networked information environment, types of information services available, how to search for information and how to make it available on the network. Library and information staff will be provided with materials to support them in training their users. A server will also be developed to include extensive network skills training packages. Developments will include CD-ROM and WWW-based tutorials, and the pilot use of video-conferencing over the network to deliver training to dispersed groups.

URL: *http://www.netskills.ac.uk*

ARIADNE

In contrast to Netskills which provides skills training, ARIADNE offers academic librarians a comprehensible digest of Internet information resources and technological developments. ARIADNE – the lead site for the project is the University of Abertay Dundee – is a bimonthly newsletter in parallel hard copy and electronic format for use over the WWW. It describes and evaluates sources and services available on the Internet of potential use to librarians.

URL: *http://ukoln.bath.ac.uk/ariadne*

SOSIG

This gateway, established in 1993 originally as an ESRC-funded project, has successfully allowed the social science research community and practitioners to discover and easily access relevant networked resources worldwide. SOSIG is an effective model for organising and exploiting subject-based Internet resources through quality control, cataloguing and classification. The service is updated regularly and is genuinely value-added. The success of the SOSIG model has spawned a handful of similar projects such as Resource Organisation and Discovery in Subject-based Services (ROADS) and Organising Medical Networked Information (OMNI).

URL: *http//sosig.ac.uk*

Although there are opportunities to acquire the techniques for searching and handling a variety of electronic sources, individual librarians need to develop their own programmes to suit their individual needs. This is referred to later in the chapter but does seem particularly relevant here since there are few commercially produced training courses that cover the complete picture. Indeed, it would be unrealistic to expect it. A number of them cover the use of the Internet or CD-ROM searching or training other users as discrete training areas.

IT Management

The technological developments in networking, electronic publishing and digitisation make it understandable that other IT-related skills are sometimes relegated to a less prominent position. The academic librarian of this decade and beyond has to possess a portfolio of other IT-related skills in order to complement and support the navigational skills. Such skills help library staff to manage the information more widely and, in turn, transfer these skills to the users as appropriate. These skills include:

- word processing
- desktop publishing
- use of bibliographic software packages
- spreadsheets
- graphics packages
- bulletin boards
- dexterity with data and file manipulation
- maintaining WWW files
- familiarity with local automated systems
- IT troubleshooting
- familiarity with different operating systems.

The library can acquire these skills through growing specialisation of skills in its staff. In institutions which have converged services or which foster close relations between library and other support staff, these skills can be acquired incrementally through locally organised training programmes.

Management skills

In Chapter 1 we outlined the importance of high quality management in ensuring that external developments are turned to the advantage of the library service. The staff who are required to adopt the skills and techniques of sound management practice will depend largely on the ethos, organisation and structure of the service. It is essential that librarians acquire the skills that will enable them to operate effectively in large and increasingly competitive organisations. In our view there is a range of factors which suggests that managerial responsibilities need to be more widely adopted. These include:

- the gradual breakdown of hierarchical staffing structures
- increasingly participative decision-making models
- greater emphasis on accountability and service or individual performance
- the growing insistence that departmental objectives support institutional strategies
- widespread financial constraints
- the importance of being able to negotiate effectively with institutional managers
- recognition that change has become a way of life
- greater emphasis on teamwork
- recognition of the importance of flexibility in working arrangements
- the devolution of responsibilities and budgets
- the importance of individual time management.

This view is reinforced in the *Fielden Report* which indicates that 'basic managerial skills are required for a range of staff' and that these should not be restricted to heads of library services. [11]

We would like to highlight three areas of management which will be of growing importance to academic librarians. They are:

- management of change
- financial management
- strategic awareness.

Management of change

It is important that changes taking place in the academic environment are treated positively and optimistically. To the cynical this may seem naive. Whenever possible, changes need to be perceived as opportunities. This philosophy, however difficult it may be for some, applies to all strata of the library service. It need not be viewed as blind acceptance of 'the way it has to be'. For example, it does not preclude the continuous striving for additional resources or the search for innovatory methods of meeting user needs. Change has to be harnessed and turned to the advantage of the service and the users. After all, what is the alternative? The service that becomes reactive to events 'outside of its control' will be driven in a direction decided by other parties who inevitably have their own planned agendas. It is easy to become part of a downward spiral in which the library receives less and less support – politically and financially – and is viewed as a 'whinging' resource-sapping central service.

Within a supportive managerial framework it is possible to reduce the resistance to change by ensuring effective channels of communication and by obtaining the commitment and involvement of the staff. Chapter 5 shows a number of examples of new services that librarians are developing as a result of changes in the delivery of teaching programmes.

Communication
This seemingly simple suggestion is the most frequent cause of failure to adapt to changing circumstances. Two-way communication is required to explain and answer questions about new services and strategies. Successful academic integration cannot be achieved without effective communication between library and academic staff in all its many forms.

Obtaining commitment and involvement
Participative management, as we indicated in Chapter 1, lies at the heart of dealing with change whether as manager or participant in the process. Whenever library staff are involved in strategic decision-making – and there is a variety of models to choose from – there is a greater chance of staff ownership and commitment. It comes as no surprise that decisions arrived at in a vacuum by a few people are often resisted by staff affected. Experience suggests that the earlier that individuals or teams are involved in decision-making, the more effective those decisions are. One way of encouraging a participative approach is to offer the type of meetings training suggested in Chapter 2.

Financial management

Increasingly, academic librarians are having to make decisions which require budgetary skills, accounting skills and techniques of economic analysis. As a result of devolved budgets, the establishment of cost centres and the internal market, many more librarians are responsible for budgets than was previously the case. The budgets may cover books, journals, furniture, IT equipment, binding, staff training, database services, document delivery services etc. Delegation of such responsibilities to subject or functional librarian has become quite common. Whilst in-depth knowledge of accountancy is unnecessary, a familiarity with both resource allocation models and the conducting of financial negotiations would be desirable.

Perhaps even more beneficial in the current climate are the skills of economic analysis. The provision of library services is becoming increasingly complex. Decisions have to be taken about the balance between different service elements for example printed v electronic, networked v stand-alone, or staffing v material. Indeed, the access and collection debate has a significant financial perspective. Technology has further muddied the economic waters for librarians generally. Careful judgements have to be made on the basis of often scant information. The variety of charging modes – subscriptions, licensing, pay-as-you-use etc – for electronic services further complicates effective financial decision-making. A rudimentary knowledge of cost-benefit analysis is becoming a necessity rather than a luxury.

The key to success in raising funds for the library lies in librarians being politically effective. Obtaining financial support is dependent upon good negotiating and political skills. These skills are identifiable and have been described by Heery and Midwinter & McVicar. [14, 15]

Strategic awareness

While it may be unnecessary for subject or faculty librarians to have well-developed strategic planning skills, it is essential that they demonstrate an awareness of matters of strategic importance to the library service. In the proactive participative service referred to above, these librarians are likely to be involved in the library's strategic decision-making process. Where this is not the case, the librarians need to show a keen awareness of:

- the institution's mission and long-term strategy
- the library's mission and strategy
- the interrelation between these two strategies
- the external environment and how it influences both institutional and library strategies
- the institutional and library planning and policy cycles.

This awareness enables the librarian to understand the context in which and the constraints under which the library service continually operates. It is sometimes easy for librarians to concentrate their attention on their own areas of responsibility and become detached from the wider picture. Academic integration, gaining credibility with the academic staff, the educational developments that underpin services to groups and individuals, cooperative ventures would all be enhanced by an awareness of strategic issues.

Responsibilities of the organisation and the individual

Ultimately, a partnership between the library and the individual librarian is the most effective means of ensuring the development of appropriate skills. Each constituent has a responsibility to the other. Benefits then accrue to the individual, the other library staff, the users and the parent institution. This partnership helps to retain the motivation of the library staff and maintain a positive attitude. For each constituent to gain maximum benefit from staff development and training there needs to be coordination and continuity.

Coordination

Staff development and training should be the formal responsibility of a senior member of staff. That person then formulates and coordinates policies across the service through consultation and discussion. The priorities for staff development and training need to reflect the strategies of the parent institution and the library. Responsibility for dispensing the staff development and training budget fairly and according to need would also lie with that member of staff. Coordination takes place in a number of ways:

- between and within different levels of staff
- bringing together collective staff development and training issues after appraisal or review
- across campuses, satellite libraries, converged services
- between in-house and externally provided events
- between individual and group events
- between assistance with qualifications and other types of events
- between institutions for example cooperative events
- between methods of staff development such as shadowing, job rotation, courses, individual study, visits, and conferences.

It is important that the coordinator has methods of identifying staff development and training needs such as staff appraisal, review, delegated representatives or committees. This information may then be taken alongside the strategic priorities to inform the decision-making process.

The coordinator can also ensure that there is consistency in the level of service provision. From this position it becomes easier to identify areas where the quality of service falls below the recognised standard and requires investigation (and possibly additional training). A good example of this is an enquiry point where the library is expected to provide an efficient and effective service regardless of the nature of the enquiry or the member of library staff who is required to answer it. Coordinated refresher and updating training sessions help to equalise competence across the service. UWE library for example has held regular staff development events – three per year – for the last five years under the coordinating eye of a member of the Library Management Team. These events organised for the sixteen subject librarians ensure that the senior staff develop skills, attitudes and services that benefit all. Not only is it an opportunity to share good practice but it also provides a check on strategic direction.

Continuity

The individual librarian is responsible for his or her own personal professional development. This may be an informal arrangement formulated by the individual and modified as the nature of the job develops and as skills are acquired. Alternatively, the process may be formalised adapting, for example, the Library Association's Framework for Continuing Professional Development. This framework is systematic but flexible so that individuals can modify it to suit their needs. The diverse range of skills required by current librarians has only been touched upon in this chapter. From the complexity of interpersonal skills training to the dynamic changes within information technology it is increasingly necessary to formalise personal professional development. This view is reinforced by Sylge: 'A personal programme of training needs to be built up by an individual as part of their working life – it is not pre-planned by an organisation'. [16]

Such programmes need to recognise the importance of updating skills. In order to maximise the benefits of staff development and training events, participants need to practice the new skills continually or apply new knowledge as soon as possible.

Increasingly, training and awareness are provided by means other than course attendance. Networking amongst librarians within and between institutions is developing rapidly. The format may be informal, conferencing, single issues or electronic newsletters. The Internet continues to gain in popularity and userfriendliness and provides the main vehicle for national and international networking. It can also be an antidote to professional isolation from which some academic librarians suffer. The establishment of a web of contacts has always loomed large in more specialised library services but information technology has made this available to a wider range of constituents.

It is important that the skills highlighted in this final chapter and those outlined in any staff development and training policies are integrated into the fabric of the service. These skills and competences should form a consistent thread through recruitment, selection, induction, on the basis of need and through the appraisa and review process.

Conclusion

We in the academic library profession are living in exciting times. It is not just the speed of change which provides the excitement but the recognition that we can make a significant contribution to the progress of the academic community. We must continue to develop our organisational, interpersonal (in the broadest sense) and IT-based skills and apply them to the people/information interface. We need to embrace innovation, eschew modesty and display what Bean describes as 'constructive arrogance'. [15] Our approach to meeting the information needs of the early twenty-first century requires us to be positive, proactive, participative and professional. Our main purpose in writing this book has been to offer a practical contribution to making this possible.

References

1. Piggott, S.E.A. The virtual library: almost there... *Special Libraries*, Fall, 1993, pp.206–212.

2. Heseltine, R. Vices and virtues in the virtual library. *Times Higher Education Supplement*, 14 October (Multimedia section), 1994, pp.IV–V.

3. Stoll, C. *Silicon snake oil: second thoughts on the information highway*. New York: Doubleday, 1995.

4. Ratcliffe, F.W. Preservation and scholarship in libraries. *Library Review*, 40(2/30), 1991, pp.6–71.

5. Heseltine, R. The challenge of learning in cyberspace. *Library Association Record, 97 (8)*, 1995, pp.432-433.

6. National Board of Employment, Education and Training. *Library provision in higher education institutions*. Canberra, Australia: NBEET, 1990 (Ross Report).

7. House, D. and Moon, C. The new university librarian. *in* Harris, C., ed. *The new university library: issues for the '90s and beyond*. London: Taylor Graham, 1994, pp.73–88.

8. Mitchell, W.B. and Morton, B. On becoming faculty librarians: acculturation problems and remedies. *College & Research Libraries,* 53(5), 1992 pp.379–392.

9. Krompart, J. Research Notes: researching faculty status: a selective annotated bibliography. *College & Research Libraries,* 53(5) 1992, pp.439–449.

10. Major, J. A. Mature librarians and the university faculty: factors contributing to librarians' acceptance as colleagues. *College & Research Libraries,* 54(6), 1993 pp.46-469.

11. Fielden, J, Supporting expansion: *a report on human resource management in academic libraries for the joint funding councils' Libraries Review Group*.Bristol: HEFCE, 1993 (Fielden Report).

12. *Libraries and IT: working papers of the Information Technology Sub-committee of the HEFCs' Libraries Review*. Bath: United Kingdom Online Network, 1993.

13. Hodges, L. Content with a starring role. *Times Higher Education Supplement,* 13 October, (Multimedia section), 1995, pIX.

14. Heery, M. Winning funds without losing friends. *Library Manager* 1, 1994, pp.9–10.

15.   Midwinter, A. and McVicar, M. The public librarians as budget manager. Journal of Librarianship and Information Science, 23(1), 1991 pp.9–20.

16.   Sylge, C. Your investment is you: personal professional and career development in the 90s. *Managing Information,* 2(10), 1995, pp.30–32.

17.   Bean, E. S. Polish up your image. *Catholic Library World*, 58(5), 1987, pp.232–236.

8. Further Reading

Chapter 1

Corrall, S. Flat structures: how low can you go? *Library Manager*, 5, 1995 pp.9–10.

Fowell, S and Levy, P. Developing a new professional practice: a model for networked learner support in higher education. *Journal of Documentation*, 51(3), 1995 pp.271–280.

Harris, C., *ed. The new university library: issues for the '90's and beyond: essays in honour of Ian Rogerson*. London: Taylor Graham, 1994.

Libraries and IT: working papers of the Information Technology Sub-committee of the HEFCs' Libraries Review. Bath: United Kingdom Online NETWORK, 1993.

Hobrock, B. G. Creating your library's future through effective strategic planning. *Journal of Library Administration*, 14(3), 1991, pp.37–57.

Line, M. Academic libraries: a new generation? Line, M., *Academic library management*. London: Library Association, 1990, pp.255–263.

Noon, P. Librarians as managers: a different set of skills? *Library Management,* 12(5), 1991, pp.4-12.

Ojala, M. Core competences for special library managers of the future. *Special Libraries*, Fall 1993, pp.230–234.

Chapter 2

Hardesty, L. Role of the classroom faculty in bibliographic instruction. in Clark, A.S. and Jones, K.F., *eds. Teaching librarians to teach: on-the-job training for bibliographic instruction librarians*. Metuchen, New Jersey: Scarecrow Press, 1986, pp.155–187.

Hodgson, P. *Effective meetings*. London: Century Business, 1992.

Sharman, D. *The perfect meeting*. London: Century Business, 1993.

Shirato, L., *ed. Working with faculty in the new electronic library*. Ann Arbor, Michigan: Pierian Press, 1992.

Widdicombe, C. *Group meetings that work: a practical guide for working with different kinds of groups*. Slough: St. Pauls, 1994.

Chapter 3

Bluck, R., Hilton, A., Noon, P. *Information skills in academic libraries: a teaching and learning role in higher education*. Birmingham: Staff and Educational Development Association, 1994.

Gibbs, G. and Jenkins, A., *eds. Teaching large classes in higher education: how to maintain quality with reduced resources.* London: Kogan Page, 1992.

Gibbs, G., Rust, C., Jenkins, A .and Jaques, D. *Developing students' transferable skills.* Oxford: Oxford Centre for Staff Development, 1994.

Hardesty,L.,*User instruction in academic libraries* Metuchen, NJ: Scarecrow Press, 1986.

Jaques, D. *Learning in groups,* 2nd ed. London: Kogan Page, 1991.

Morrison, M and Markless, S. *Enhancing information skills in further education: some strategies for senior mangers, lectures and librarians.* London: British Library, 1992. (BL Research Paper no.99)

Race, P. and Brown, S. *500 tips for tutors.* London: Kogan Page, 1993

Shirato, L., *ed. What is good instruction now? library instruction for the 90s.* Ann Arbor, Michigan: Pierian Press, 1993.

Weiss, S. C. The impact of electronic tools on the four-step approach to library research. *Research Strategies,* 12(4), 1994, pp.243–6.

Chapter 4

Butler, J. T. A current awareness service using microcomputer databases and e-mail. *College and Research Libraries,* 54(2), 1993 pp.115–123.

Hay, F. J. The subject specialist in the academic library: a review article. *Journal of Academic Librarianship,* 16(1), 1990 pp.11-17.

Jackaman, P. *Basic reference and information work,* 2nd ed. Huntingdon: ELM Publications, 1989.

Kinder, R. *Librarians on the Internet: impact on reference services.* Binghampton, New York: Haworth Press, 1994.

Mardikian, J. and Kesselman, M. Beyond the desk: enhanced reference staffing for the electronic library. *Reference Services Review,* 23(1),1995, pp.21-28.

Roes, H. Current awareness services at Tilburg University. *The Electronic Library,* 11(2) 1993, pp.99 –103.

Rowley, J. Revolution in current awareness services. *Journal of Library and Information Science,* 26(1), 1994, pp.7–14.

Webb, S. *Preparing a guide to your library and information service.* London: Aslib, 1995.

Chapter 5

Brophy, P. Distant libraries: the support of higher education students who study off-campus. *Library Management,* 13(6), 1992, pp.4–7.

Clarke, H. Academic library services for students with disabilities. *Library and Information Reserch News,* 19(62), Spring 1995, pp.10-17.

Fisher, R. K. Off-campus library services in higher education in the United Kingdom. *Library Trends,* 19(62), Spring 1991, pp.479–94.

Jolly, J. Distance learning support: quality support for distance learning students. *ELG News*, Summer 1995, pp.4-6.

Kascus, M. and Aguilar, W. Providing library support to off-campus programs. *College & Research Libraries*, 49(1), 1988, pp.29–37.

O'Donohoe, S. *et al.* Mature students: counselling and guidance needs – a role for libraries and learning resources providers. *Learning Resources Journal,* 8(2), 1992, pp.40–43.

Tooby, B. Library services for disabled users at the University of the West of England. *SCONUL Newsletter, No.4,* Spring 1995, pp.46–47.

Chapter 6

Baker, D. Access versus holdings policy with special reference to the University of East Anglia. *Interlending and Document Supply,* 20(4), 1992, pp.131-137.

Blunden-Ellis, J. The Consortium of Academic Libraries in Manchester (CALIM): strategic and development planning of a new consortium. *Publications of Essen University Library, 17,* 1994, pp.99–114.

Hart, Liz. A time for cooperation? *Library Manager* No.10, 1995, p5.

Heaney, H. J. Cooperation in collections. in Line, M. *ed. Academic library management.* London: Library Association, 1990, pp.147–154.

Jurrow, S. and Webster, D. E. Building new futures for research libraries. *Journal of Library Administration,* 14(2), 1991 pp.5–19.

Line, M. Preserving the eternal values of the research library in a throwaway age. *Library Review,* 40(2/3), 1991. pp.44–51.

MacDougall, A.F. Other forms of cooperation. in Line, M., *ed.. Academic Library Management.* London: Library Association, 1990, pp.155–159.

Ratcliffe, F. W. and Foskett, D. J. The consortium of university research libraries (CURL): a new cooperative venture in the United Kingdom. *British Journal of Academic Librarianship,* 4(1), 1989, pp.1-18.

Chapter 7

British Journal of Academic Librarianship, 9(3), 1994 is a special issue devoted to *Fielden Report* and human resource management.

Jordan, P. *Staff management in library and information work.* 3rd edition. Aldershot: Gower, 1995.

Leach, K. Evaluating the use of electronic networking for continuing professional development. *Library and Information Research News,* 19(63), 1995, pp.22–25.

Levy, P. *Interpersonal skills.* London: Library Association Publishing, 1993.

McKay, D. *Effective financial planning for library and information services.* London: Aslib, 1995.

Mayon-White, B., *ed. Planning and managing change.* London: Harper and Row, 1986.

Roberts, N. and Kohn, T. *Librarians and professional status.* London: Library Association, 1991.

Saunders, L.M., ed. *The virtual library: visions and realities.* Westport, Connecticut: Meckler, 1992.

Tseng, G., Poulter, A. and Hiom, D. *The library and information professional's guide to the Internet.* London: Library Association Publishing, 1995.

Appendix I

Meeting Audit – Feedback Questionnaire

Meeting: .... Date: ....

Chairperson: ....

Mark each of the following statements on a scale 1 (disagree completely) to 5 (agree completely). Avoid using 3 unless you are genuinely neutral.

Section 1   **disagree**   **agree**

1. The meeting was necessary   1 2 3 4 5
2. The objectives of the meeting were clear   1 2 3 4 5
3. The meeting achieved its objectives   1 2 3 4 5
4. The meeting was the right length   1 2 3 4 5
5. The meeting was held at a convenient time 1 2 3 4 5
6. The meeting started and finished on time   1 2 3 4 5
8. The venue was comfortable   1 2 3 4 5

Section 2

9. There was sufficient notice of the meeting 1 2 3 4 5
10. The agenda was distributed in good time   1 2 3 4 5
11. The agenda was sufficiently detailed   1 2 3 4 5
12. All papers were distributed with the agenda 1 2 3 4 5

Section

13. The meeting followed the agenda   1 2 3 4 5
14. The chairperson controlled the meeting well 1 2 3 4 5
15. Time keeping was good   1 2 3 4 5
16. Everyone was encouraged to participate   1 2 3 4 5
17. The decision making process was satisfactory 1 2 3 4 5
18. Decisions were the result of consensus   1 2 3 4 5
19. Responsibility for action was clear   1 2 3 4 5

Section 4

20. Minutes were circulated properly   1 2 3 4 5
21. Minutes were accurate   1 2 3 4 5
22. Minutes were clear   1 2 3 4 5

Please return your completed form to the chairperson of your meeting.

This questionnaire is adapted by permission of Burrington Partnership 1995.

Appendix II

University of the West of England, Bristol – Continuing Education Unit

Teaching and Learning in the Library Environment

Handouts:

Why take trouble with them?

-
-

Factors to consider: Content. Design. Presentation.

Contents:

What are the purposes of the handouts you use?

-
-

Give some examples ... specific, structured, shorts, same heading

Design:

Why is it important to take care with the design of handouts?

-
-

Presentation: What are the issues around when and how you present handouts to your students?

Your Own Notes and Comments:

-
-

Interactive handouts

-
-

Other examples

Appendix III

User Education Log

Course/programme: module year

Staff contact: ext. date booked

Students per session: * no. of sessions =

Length of session: * no. of sessions =

	Date	Time	Room	Equipment
1.	....	....	....	....
2.	....	....	....	....
3.	....	....	....	....
4.	....	....	....	....
5.	....	....	....	....
6.	....	....	....	....

Aims/objectives

Content

Evaluation

(Attach student assignment and library handouts used)

Appendix IV

Induction Set Up Sheet

Name of Event:
Course Title: FT/PT:
Date: Time: Location:
Numbers: No. of Groups: Per Group:
Personnel Required:

Venue
Set up required: Classroom   Cafe   Other

Equipment needed:
Network   Online   Standalone   Video   Other

Equipment to be booked:
OPACs   Levels:
Network PCs   Levels:
Standalone CDs:
Online databases:

Paperwork
Signs to be produced by: Completed?
Registration forms: Course No:
Other programmes:

Handouts
Handouts required:
Collation required?   Done by:
Completed?   Room to be set up at: by:

Notes:

Programme   *Bolland Library*
Date   *Business Team*

156

Appendix V

Programme ....

Date ....

LIBRARY EVALUATION SHEET

I would appreciate it if you would take a couple of minutes at the end of your library seminar/workshop to complete this evaluation sheet. It would help me in planning future library sessions.

Please circle or tick the answer which most closely matches your feelings.

1. **Did you find the length of the session:**

    Too long   Just right   Too short

2. **Was the content appropriate to your needs?**

    Yes, very   OK   Not at all

    If not, please comment ....

    ....

3. **Did you feel you had gained useful knowledge by participating?**

    Yes, lots   OK   No, not enough

    If not, please comment ....

    ....

4. **Was the session aimed at the right level?**

    Too complicated   OK   Too simplistic

5. **Was the material clearly presented?**

    Very well   OK   Not very well

    If not, please comment ....

    ....

    P.T.O.

6. **Did the session come at the right stage in the module?**

Too soon   About right   Too late

7. **Was the size of the group:**

Too large   About right   Too small

8. **Would you have liked more tuition in any of the sections covered:**

Literature searching   Y/N If yes please expand.................................

....

CD-ROMs   Y/N If yes please expand.................................

....

On-line databases   Y/N If yes please expand.................................

....

Anything else   Y/N If yes please expand.................................

....

9. **Do you have any further comments about this session?**...............................

....

Many thanks for your co-operation.

Jan Nichols / Jackie Chelin
Business School Librarians
Room 5D11, ext. 2446

158

Appendix VI

UWE Library Services – Customer Care Statement

- We will base present and future services on the needs of our customers
- We will plan our services realistically and deploy resources where most needed
- We endeavour at all times to be approachable, to be courteous and helpful, and to treat our customers with respect
- We aim to run our services in an efficient, effective and professional manner
- Each of our customers is entitled to spend time with appropriate library staff concerning his or her information or service needs
- We will listen to the comments of our customers
- We aim to ensure high quality customer service by encouraging and providing appropriate development and training of all library staff
- We will endeavour to keep customers and colleagues informed of library activities, policies and developments

Library Policy Committee

Appendix VII

Readers' Enquiries

Referral/Action

Service Point: ....

Member of staff: ....

Date/time: ....

User name: ....

Registration no: ....

Course/Department: ....

Tel no: ....

Address: ....

....

E-mail address: ....

....

Details of enquiry: ....

....

....

Background details: ....

....

Level of information: ....

....

When required ....

....

For Office Use

Appendix VIII

User Interest Profile

Name of academic staff, group, research unit: ....

Department: ....

Person to contact: ....

Position: ....

Room no: ....

Tel no: ....

Fax no: ....

E-mail address: ....

Subject Interests *(Please indicate whether research, teaching or other)*:

....

....

Electronic/printed sources scanned/used regularly:

....

....

Membership of lists, associations etc:

....

Availability of computing facilities:

....

Date of profile: ....

Signed: (1) ....

            (2) ....

Updated: ....

Appendix IX

ECONOMICS AND SOCIAL SCIENCE

Monthly List of New Books and Contents Pages

Evaluation Sheet

Every month you receive a copy of the Economics and Social Science Bulletin indicating new books bought for the library and the contents pages of relevant journals. The purpose of this brief questionnaire is to find out your views on its usefulness.

(1) Which School are you in?

ECON   ☐   HUMS   ☐
POL   ☐   OTHER
SOC   ☐

(2) Do you receive your own copy regularly?   Y ☐
  N ☐

(3) If you do not receive a copy but would like to, please write your name

....

(4) If you receive a copy but do not wish to, please write your name

....

(5) Do you scan
the list of new books?
the journal contents pages?
both? ☐

(6) Is it helpful for the book list to be
in one alphabetical sequence?
divided into subject areas? ☐

(7) *How often do you seek out a new book on the list?*

        every bulletin
        every other bulletin
        other

(8) *How often do you follow up a journal issue from the contents pages?*

        every bulletin
        every other bulletin
        other

(9) *Do you use the bulletin to*

        help compile reading lists?
        refer items to students?
        help with your research interests?
        if other, please specify

        ....

(10) *Would you scan the list of new books if it was e-mailed to you rather than sent to you in printed format?* Y N

Thank you for completing the evaluation. Please could you return it in the internal mail.

Many thanks.

Steve Morgan

Appendix X

University of the West of England, Bristol – Information for Students on part-time and Distance Learning Courses

Bolland Library
Welcome to the library service of the University of the West of England. This booklet sets out the library services offered to students on part-time and distance learning courses and will help you to make efficient use of the library. All students enrolled on courses at UWE are able to join the library and use the facilities of the four university campus libraries. This means that it is not necessary for you to return library books to the campus you borrowed them from. You can always return them to the campus most convenient to you.

Registration
A library registration form must be completed before you use any of the library services. This can be done in person or by post if necessary. Proof of course registration is required. You will need to do this before you can use any of the library services.

Advisor to Part-time Students
This is a service which aims to provide support for students on part-time and distance learning courses. SB is the Advisor to Part-time Students and may be contacted from 11.00 am - 1.00 pm and 3.00 - 5.00 pm Mondays to Fridays, either in person or by telephone. Her desk is situated on level 2 opposite the main issue desk. The direct telephone line is 000 000 0000 and fax 000 000 0000. If you ring outside these hours, you may leave a message on the telephone answering service or there is a box on the desk for personal callers to leave messages.

Additional services for part-time and distance learning students

Phone renewals
You may phone to renew library books twice providing that they have not been reserved by another student. It is not possible to renew medium loan books. Please remember that fines are charged if books are returned to the library late. The charges are shown in the Bolland Library Guide.

Holding books for collection
You may phone to reserve books which will be held for you to collect from the issue desk. Books that are on loan when you ring may also be reserved. A notice will be sent to you when these books are available for collection. Up to ten days are given for reserved books to be collected. It is not possible to post books to students.

Photocopies
At any one time you may request up to 10 journal articles or chapters from books held at the library to be photocopied for you. Visitors to the library are normally expected to photocopy items themselves. It is possible to post items to students living within a radius of over 10 miles from the university. The UK law of copyright is strictly adhered to. This means that users are able to photocopy the whole or part of a single article from an issue of a journal or up to 5% or one chapter of a book providing it is for private research or study. Photocopies are charged at the rate of 5p per sheet. Payment can be made by cheque. Please make cheques payable to UWE, Bristol, and give bank cheque card details on the reverse of the cheque. It is necessary to sign a copyright declaration which must be signed and returned to the library. Please give at least 3 days' notice of any photocopying required. This does not include time for items to be sent to you by post.

Interlibrary Loans
Books and journals which are not in stock in the University library may be obtained from another library. When requesting items, please give as much accurate information as possible. For books, it is necessary to give details of author, title, date, publisher, and ISBN number and for journal articles, author and title of the article, the title of the journal, year of publication, volume, part and page numbers. It can take up to 2 weeks or longer for material to arrive, so it is important to take this into account when you plan your work. Books borrowed from other libraries must be collected in person, photocopies can be posted on to you. As this is an expensive service for the library, certain restrictions have had to be made. It is possible for students to have up to 10 concurrent requests. One interlibrary loan form needs to be completed for each item and requests have to be countersigned by your Subject Librarian. If you are not able to visit the library in person, forms may be sent to Sue Baldwin, who will obtain signatures for you. British Library copyright declaration forms must be signed and returned to the library.

Electronic Services
The library subscribes to over thirty CD-ROM and Online databases. The terminals are often in heavy use and it is necessary to book a time which is convenient for you to access a particular database. Not all terminals are connected to printers and it is advisable to bring a 3 1/2-inch disk so that you are able to download information.

Appointments
It is possible for Sue to make an appointment for you to see your subject librarian. Please note: At present we are unable to post books to students. We would remind you that you are responsible for all books issued on your library card. If you wish to return books to the library by post, please remember that you are responsible for all books issued on your ticket. We strongly advise you to return all books by recorded delivery.

Remote access to the library catalogue
It is possible to access the library catalogue and other services from outside the library using a modem. A guide to the remote dial-in procedure is available on request. SB may be contacted by E-mail (xxx@uwe.ac.uk). Uncover is a service which is available via Janet and gives the contents pages of over 15,000 journals on all subjects. It is possible to order articles from this service using your personal credit card.

Loss of card and change of address
Please report the loss of your library card to the library as soon as possible. A charge of £1.00 is made for replacement cards. For the efficient running of the above service, it is important that you inform the library of any changes to your address or telephone numbers. It is necessary to inform the library as well as your Faculty as students' records are maintained independently by the library.

Part-time loan books
Books in the library have different loan periods. The loan periods are described in the Guide to the Bolland Library. Copies of essential texts are often available for part-time students only to borrow. These are distinguished by the letters "PT" on the spine and a blue band around the book. Part-time loan books are available for 3 weeks and may be renewed twice providing they have not been reserved by another borrower.

Enquiry service
An enquiry service operates on level 3 of the Bolland library during library opening hours. Qualified members of staff are available to help if you have any queries. They will also be able to help with basic IT queries.

Photocopiers
Photocopiers are available on each floor of the library. It is possible to enlarge and reduce copies and some of the photocopiers will give A3 copies. There are no colour photocopying facilities available in the library. Each copy costs 5p per sheet. Students may buy a flexicard from dispensers on levels 3 and 5 of the library. A flexicard costs £1.00 and may be re-charged with 50p or £1 coins. There are also some coin operated photocopiers. It is important that you bring

change with you, as there are limited facilities available in the library for giving change. It is possible to copy from microfiche and microfilm in the library. Some of the equipment takes flexicards and some are coin operated only. It is necessary to book a time which is convenient to use this equipment.

Services for disabled students
The Bolland Library is on four floors and there is a lift in the library to all floors. Services for disabled students are provided by BT (ext. 0000) and MS (ext. 0000). A CCTV and PC with scanner, voice synthesiser and braille embosser are available in the library for use by blind and partially sighted students.

Book return box
There is a box outside the library for returned library books. It is possible to leave library books in this box when the library is closed. The building is open from 6.30 am on Mondays-Fridays. The building is not open after the library closes at 9.00 pm or outside library opening hours at weekends.

Subject Librarians
Each Faculty has its own Subject Librarian, Bristol Business School and the Faculty of the Built Environment have two. Subject Librarians are specialists in the information sources of their particular subject area. Subject Librarians liaise closely with teaching staff in the Faculties to ensure that students receive training in using the resources available in their subject area. If you have a specific subject enquiry or would like help in researching a particular topic, it is possible to make an appointment to see your Subject Librarian either directly or through SB.

The following guides are enclosed:
A Guide to the Bolland Library - this includes details of library opening hours, loan periods and fines.

Rules and regulations.

Your four libraries - this gives details of the addresses and phone numbers of all campus libraries.

The following guides are available on application:
AV Guide - guide to the audio-visual collection.

More than just a catalogue! - details of how to use the library computerised catalogue.

Remote dial-in to the library catalogue.

Appendix XI

Guide to Library Services for Distance Learners – Northern College of Education (Aberdeen Campus)

Welcome to the College Library Service
Northern College, as you probably know, has two campuses, at Aberdeen and Dundee. These notes relate to the Aberdeen Campus only and can usefully be read in conjunction with the general Guide to Library Services which is included in this information package. It is important to remember that although you are studying at a distance from College the full range of Library services is available to you. The Senior Librarian (User Services), JJ, is your contact person for this purpose and she should be able to answer any questions you may have. Her direct dial telephone number is 000 000 0000, and if she's not immediately available, other members of the Library staff will help as much as possible.

Hours of opening and telephone numbers
During term time the Library is open between 8.45 am and 9.30 pm from Monday to Friday, and from 9.30 am to 12.30 pm on Saturday. In the vacations, hours of opening are 9.00 am to 5 pm only, Monday to Friday. With the rest of the College, the Library is closed for two weeks over Christmas and New Year. The summer vacation lasts from late June to the end of September. The direct dial telephone number for general enquiries is 000 000 0000.

Registering as a Borrower
In many cases, Course tutors will issue library registration cards for you to complete and may even return them to us on your behalf. If you haven't received such a card and need material, don't worry. Write, telephone or fax, and we'll enclose one when the required items are sent out to you. Please read the Library Regulations, then fill in the necessary details on your registration card and return it to the Library as soon as possible. You will be issued with 12 green tickets, valid until the end of your course. With each of these you can borrow one book, journal or audio-visual item, or 3 pictures. Tickets for Distance Learning students are normally kept in the Library to facilitate borrowing arrangements. If you make a personal visit to the Library, you need to advise the Issue Desk staff accordingly, so that any material you want to take away can be issued to you.

168

Borrowing Arrangements

The normal loan period is 4 weeks, but lending arrangements are much more flexible for members of distance learning (including mixed-mode) courses for teachers, social workers and community education staff. During the summer vacation, you should receive a list giving details of all items on loan to you, and you could also expect to receive a general reminder letter at Christmas and Easter, asking you to return any items no longer required and to renew those you wish to keep out on loan. If you do renew a loan by letter or telephone, it's helpful if you give your name and course, and it's essential that you quote the accession number (stamped on the book pocket or above the date label) of the book or other material, e.g. 48785, 150296, C2345, K678, plus the last date stamped on the date label. Please try not to retain library material for any longer than you need it. Other members of College courses may require the same items for their studies. When a book is in particular demand, it will probably be issued to you on a short loan only, e.g. 1 week, 2 weeks. It is very helpful if you can return that item to us as soon as possible, but we do know that time will be taken in transit and we make due allowance for it. You can also let us know if you wish to reserve the item again, if you haven't completely finished with it. If there are any problems with short-loan items, do tell us, please, so that we can make arrangements to cope with them. The same applies if you receive a postcard clearly marked Special Recall, which asks you to return an item for a specific purpose, but do please try to comply with the request as soon as possible. When your course is completed, all library material must be returned to the College Library. Please remember that we send invoices to those borrowers who do not return items within a reasonable period of time. If you want to continue using the Library after the end of your course, it is possible that you will be eligible to register as a Subscription Borrower. Please ask for more details if you are interested in this category of Library membership.

How to Get the Information you Require

If you know the books/material you require, maybe you can make a personal visit to the Library to collect them for yourself. Alternatively, you can write, telephone (000 000 0000), or fax us (000 000 0000) giving the author and title of each item. Those immediately available will be posted to you, and items on loan can be reserved and recalled for you if you wish. It's helpful if you can tell us the latest date by which an item is required, and we'll try to get it to you in good time. This may involve borrowing from other libraries (Inter-Library Loans) and if something is sent to you in this way, you must comply with the loan period information given on the yellow slip enclosed in the book. Failure to do so may mean that the lending library will refuse to let us borrow in the future. Please note that the College will pay the cost of postage to you, but you will have to pay the return postage yourself, or you could, perhaps, return items via your tutor. Sometimes you may be able to get the material you want more quickly by using your local public library or school resources service; it's worth exploring these possibilities. If your course-work entails a study where the details of relevant books are unknown to you, we can try to find information for you. This also applies if all the books you want are on loan and there may be a delay before we can send them to you. You can ask JJ to "send me something on ...", and in such cases it helps if you can:

- give as much information as possible about what you want.

- state the level of information you require, e.g. a simple statement of facts, or a more detailed analysis.

- say if the material should be aimed for use in primary or secondary schools, or with a particular age group.

- This is particularly important! Is it, for example, primary (early stages, upper primary), secondary, 5-14, 10-14, post-16, etc.? give a brief idea of what you've consulted already.

- indicate the deadline for receiving the information.

It's most important, too, to give us as much time as possible to look out the information for you and obviously, with such enquiries, it's better if you talk or write to Jean personally. If you telephone and she's not immediately available, other members of the Library staff may be able to help, but will probably take a note of your requirements and pass them on to her. So that she can get back to you if necessary, it's useful to have a contact number; this applies if you write or fax too.

Do remember that we want to be of as much help to you as possible. If you need any more information about services available to you, please contact:

JJ, Senior Librarian (User Services) or CS-B, Principal Librarian, Northern College, Aberdeen Campus, Hilton Place, Aberdeen AB9 1FA, Tel: 000 000 0000 Fax: 000 000 0000.

Appendix XII

AULIC Staff Exchange and Work Shadowing Scheme – University libraries of Bath, Bristol and UWE

Introduction

1. Definitions

    1.1 A staff exchange involves two members of staff carrying out each others' jobs for a period of time. An exchange would normally be for a minimum of one month and those involved would not spend time together (except perhaps for a brief hand-over period).

    1.2 Work shadowing involves a member of staff spending a period of time with another member of staff in order to learn all about the other person's job and how it is performed. Work shadowing would not normally last more than one week.

2. Scope

Staff at any level are entitled to participate in staff exchange or shadowing schemes, provided an opposite number with the appropriate skills is willing and able to participate. These guidelines are specifically limited to the institutions which are members of AULIC.

3. Aims of the scheme

The aims of the exchange and shadowing scheme are:

- to enable staff at all levels to extend their work experience.

- to benefit the institutions involved by encouraging exchanges of experience, ideas and good practice.

4. Initiating the exchange or job shadowing

Any member of staff wishing to undertake an exchange or shadow another person should first discuss the matter with their manager and the Deputy Librarian (Personnel). Detailed guidelines are attached. Further guidelines for the library hosting such a visit are available on request. Participating staff will be entitled to the same facilities and opportunities as their counterparts. For example, induction programmes, mentors and staff development activities should be offered to staff on exchange schemes.

JP, CS, AT.

Guidelines for the visitor

1. Preparation for Visit

1.1 Discuss your proposal with your manager and with the Deputy Librarian (Personnel), to get approval.

1.2 You should discuss matters such as:

- how long the visit should be and when it might take place.

- travel arrangements

- aims of the visit - what do you expect to get from it.

- whether you wish to shadow an individual or make an exchange.

- which library you would like to work in.

- whether you have had any previous contact with staff in the library.

- any problems about hours of work or time of arrival at the library.

1.3 The Deputy Librarian (Personnel) will then contact the library you have chosen to see if an appropriate placement can be arranged.

1.4 If the proposal is accepted, it might be necessary for you to make a preliminary visit to discuss matters further, but this would not always be necessary under the shadowing scheme. It will be much more important to make a visit if you are considering an exchange arrangement, as you will have to discuss all the implications of the work with your opposite number.

1.5 When the Deputy Librarian (Personnel) has made the arrangement, she will write formally to the library you will be visiting giving details about you, including background information on your experience, length of visit, any duties you will be expected to undertake, and any special requirements you may have.

1.6 The host Staff Development Officer will then write to you confirming the arrangements and providing you with information about directions to the library, who to report to on the first day, and at what time.

2. *The first day of your exchange or shadowing period*

2.1 You will meet the Staff Development Officer and be introduced to the person you are shadowing, or the Section or Department head of the team. You will be given details such as:

- lockers/coats/bag accommodation
- meals and break times
- an introduction to library staff
- a tour of the library
- general information about the library and institution and campus area
- reporting procedure in case of sickness.

2.2 The first day will generally be a settling in time and you may not see too much of the actual job.

3. *During the shadowing or exchange*

3.1 In the first day or two you should establish with your opposite number/supervisor full details of what you would like to do, and how far this can be met.

3.2 It is expected that part of the time you may be merely observing, but it is likely that for your own benefit, and that of the library, you will do a certain amount of practical work. This will be left for you to work out, as the needs of the library will have to be considered. Remember that it may not be possible for you to do everything you would like to do.

3.3 Nevertheless, it is important that you should get as much out of this placement as possible, and you will be treated very much as though you were a member of the library's staff. You should therefore take the initiative in asking questions and finding out as much as possible about the job.

3.4 If you are taking part in an exchange, you will have worked out in advance with your opposite number details of your duties and you will be expected to become a normal working member of the library as soon as possible. The Staff Development Officer will give you any help you require.

4. *End of visit*

4.1 On your last day or so, you should arrange a suitable time to discuss with your opposite number/supervisor how the placement has gone and any matters relating to it that you would like to raise. Staff on exchange visits may like to discuss this period of work with the host Staff Development Officer.

4.2 After you have returned to your own library, you will be expected to write a report (one side of A4) on the placement. In this you should say what you think you have achieved and put forward any comments or suggestions for any improvements you think would be useful.

4.3 This report should be given to the Deputy Librarian (Personnel) who will send a copy to the Staff Development Officer of the host library.

Guidelines for the Host Library

1. Staff at the host library

The appropriate member(s) of staff (Staff Development Officers, Department heads, etc.) at the host library should pay attention to the following points, in consideration of the individual being shadowed or participating in an exchange, and other members (if any) of the same department.

1.1 Explain and discuss the purpose of the shadowing or exchange exercise with the relevant host staff with reference to the host's and visitor's objectives.

1.2 Ensure host staff are aware of the length of the shadowing or exchange exercise.

1.3 Ensure host staff are aware of what has to be covered, how much observation *v* practical experience to offer the visiting staff, and what, if any, transactions the visiting staff may not undertake, and why not.

1.4 Pass on background details about the visitor, such as relevant experience, position in organisation, etc.

1.5 Ensure all library staff have been made aware that there will be a visitor, and of the purpose and duration of the visit.

1.6 Discuss shadowing or exchange experience after the visitor has left; what has host learned about role, about library service, other services, other work practices, etc.

1.7 Report, as applicable, to other members of the library staff on the shadowing or exchange experience.

2. The visitor(s) at the host library

The appropriate member(s) of staff (Staff Development Officers, Department heads etc.) at the host library should pay attention to the following points in consideration of the visitor(s).

2.1 Explain usual working hours and other relevant domestic arrangements including toilets, breaks, where to leave coats and bags, and campus facilities. Provide details of basic health and safety procedure, e.g. fire alarms.

2.2 Ensure the visitor knows whom to contact in case of sickness or other personal problems.

2.3 Ensure the visitor is aware of the length of the shadowing or exchange exercise.

2.4 Explain and discuss the purpose of the shadowing or exchange exercise for the host and the visitor.

2.5 Give the visitor sufficient background information about the library and the specific department/section to enable them to put their experience into the context of the information service as a whole, e.g. discuss the objectives of the parent organisation, the library and the department.

2.6 Explain the hows, whys and wherefores of each element of work - do not just do it.

2.7 Encourage the visitor to ask questions. Answer them as fully as possible, and refer to the reporting officer in case of doubt.

2.8 Encourage the visitor to do as much practical work as is feasible. If necessary, explain why they cannot do certain elements.

2.9 As far as is reasonable, introduce the visitor to staff encountered during the normal course of work and briefly explain their role in the library.

2.10 In the case of shadowing, if the person being shadowed has to leave unexpectedly, or suddenly take time off work, warn the visitor and ensure that they know whom to shadow instead.

2.11 Discuss shadowing or exchange experience with the visitor(s) towards the end of the visit.

2.12 Remember, it is all strange, and possibly extremely bewildering to the visitor.

Appendix XIII

Library Services – Financial Estimates 1996-97

These estimates are in three parts, covering the needs of:

1. The four existing UWE libraries in their present configuration.
2. The four new health libraries.
3. The Bolland Library extension.

1. Introduction

The paper recognises the serious nature of the financial situation facing the University. It therefore suggests how the Library can help in making savings. At the same time the University must appreciate that use of the library services is continuing to grow steadily. Periodicals prices also continue to rise very sharply. Both the growth in use of the library and the inflation rate for periodicals reduce the effectiveness of the Library's budget, before any cut in it is made.

1.1 Growth in use

1995-96 saw the University undertake a major TLSDC report on teaching and learning. The report found that:

"The main impact on the student experience had come from the rapid increase in student numbers and the relative decrease in the unit of resource, which had been accompanied by other factors such as the introduction of the modular scheme. The immediate response to managing the situation has been a reduction in staff / student contact hours and in many cases changes to teaching and learning approaches were a necessary consequence of this. The student experience had largely been of an increase in class size, reduction in contact hours and more emphasis on student-centred learning."

The Library is central to this shift, as it is explicitly organised so as support student learning in a environment of reduced contact with academic staff. At the strategic level the University recognises that investment in its Library is a cost-effective way of implementing the institutional teaching and learning strategy. This is recognised in the 1995-96 report on teaching and learning which commends "... The pro-active approach of the library." The consequence of the Library's development in support of student-centred learning can be seen in continuing significant growth in the use of library services.

The following figures show the percentage increase in use for each of a range of library services. The figures compare the period August 1994 – February 1995 with August 1995 – February 1996.

	Growth in use
Loans of books	5.69%
Reservations	10.73%
Interlibrary loans	24.27%
Use of LIBERTAS	14.47%
Gate counts	5.59%
Information skills teaching	36.35%

It is realistic to anticipate that cuts in faculty resources will lead to greater increase in the use of library services in 1996-97. For this reason the deans will support a measure of protection for the library budget.

1.2 Periodicals prices
Whilst book prices remain at the level of the overall inflation rate, periodicals prices continue to rise alarmingly. They have risen by 10% in 1995-96. Blackwells are predicting a 12% increase in 1996-97. The consequence of this sharp rise will be to further reduce the money available for other materials and services, as periodicals continue to absorb a larger part of the library budget.

	Expenditure on periodicals
1995-96	£580,000
1996-97	£650,000

Periodicals price rises of themselves will impose a cut of £70,000 in the Library's bookfund.